MAGNIFICENT
MORRIS MINOR

MAGNIFICENT MORRIS MINOR

MAX HORVAT

BOOKMARQUE
PUBLISHING
Minster Lovell · Oxfordshire

To all Morris Minor owners and drivers — past, present and future

First published December 1990

© Max Horvat 1990

British Library Cataloguing in Publication Data

Horvat, Max
  Magnificent Morris Minor
  1. Morris Minor cars
  I. Title
  629.2222

ISBN 1–870519–10–8

Page layout by John Rose
Edited by T. C. Colverson
Text keyed on a Linokey by Kim Giles
Typeset by Bookmarque Publishing
Set in 10½ on 13 point Souvenir
Printed on Fineblade Smooth 150gsm
Published by Bookmarque Publishing · Minster Lovell & New Yatt · Oxfordshire
Printed and bound by Butler & Tanner Ltd · Frome · Somerset

CONTENTS

ACKNOWLEDGEMENTS

For permission to enter their private property with my car for the purpose of photography I tender my most sincere thanks to:

H. M. The Queen
Rt Hon the Earl of Mansfield
Capt A. A. C. Farquharson of Invercauld
Mrs Patricia Maxwell-Scott
Mr and Mrs R. G. Reynolds

For support on the journeys abroad:
to my wife Slava, Graham Rendle, Charles Reynolds, Ernest Tavener, Mrs Joy Jones, Miss Carol Selby and to Laurie Green

For photographic assistance:
to Laurie Green and Tony Ferretti

For special car servicings over the years:
to Paul Wenzell and Paul Willson

For accepting me and my car with outstretched arms whenever I appeared dead tired in front of their door:
to Erich and Andrée Vogt, Tony and Ella Kögl-Walch, Mrs Elise Beck, Marijan and Davorin Horvat, and Ljubomir Barbić

For support on my unexpected journey to Rome:
Professor Lucedio Greci and Luigi and Angela Carletti

Photographs on front jacket and on pages 43, 57, 87, & 91:
courtesy of Laurie Green

6

PREFACE

How long is a period of thirtythree years?
In the life of the Universe or of our Earth, such a period is so minute, so infinitely short, as to have no significance. Even a millenium, they say, is hardly anything to go by. Thus in the Earth's life thirty-three years mean nothing.

In the life of a person, or a nation, a lot can, and does, happen during such a period of time. Wars may be fought, state boundaries may change, established schools of thought may lose validity and economic systems collapse. In the case of human beings a period of thirtythree years might even cover a person's life from the cradle to the grave. Thus, in people's lives thirtythree years is quite something.

For a car, however, thirtythree years is a very long period indeed. It truly borders on longevity. The life of racing cars is shortest. No sooner have they produced a crop of speed victories than they get out of date and become 'history'. For an ordinary car to perform after thirtythree years in the same way as it did at the beginning of its life is a colossal achievement, well worth putting on record.

Many books have been written about cars from the manufacturing point of view: design, prototypes, specifications, tests, colour schemes, modifications and relative merits. But once the cars leave the factory's assembly lines and land in the hands of their owners they seem to vanish into the unknown, except perhaps for short descriptions of some episodes in their lives.

This book, strictly non-fiction, non-technical and non-scientific, deals exclusively with a thirtythree years old, ordinary, mass-produced Morris Minor. Since several other books provide full technical details, all figures quoted here serve the sole purpose of providing only rough guidance.

During 1948-1971 more than 1,600,000 Morris Minors of various types were produced, of which approximately 500,000 were exported. Although production ceased in 1971, more than 200,000 of them are still happily running on British roads alone. With spare parts having become available again the Morris Minor renaissance is in full swing and there is every hope that many examples will last well into the next millenium.

This car, with its genuine and trouble-free 165,000 miles on the clock, is still running with its original engine, gearbox and transmission. During its life it has traversed this country from east to west, from south to the far north, has crossed the English Channel 27 times, in both directions, by sea or by air, has carried canoes to distant waters, has tackled almost every alpine pass in Switzerland, has visited royal castles here and abroad, has been to Rome and has looked from

7

Gibraltar over to Africa. During its first three European tours it climbed to a combined height greater than that at which the Concorde cruises. The car has all the time been in the hands of one owner and all its journeys have been carefully logged.

There will hardly be a motorist with several long-distance tours to his credit who will not at some stage in this book say: "I was here... and here... and here." This book is intended to give special pleasure and encouragement to all past and present Morris Minor owners and/or drivers; and to many more.

1957 — CHOOSING THE CAR

The year 1957 belonged to the period of the rather lean postwar years when the country was still in the process of being rebuilt. Industry was geared for export to earn foreign currency so urgently needed for buying raw materials. Moderation and simplicity were the guiding principles and new cars were difficult to obtain: the quota allocated to dealers for sale on the home market was small and always quickly exhausted.

Whilst toying with the idea of buying a car I came to the conclusion that a car capable of going from 0–60 in 10 seconds was exactly the car I did not want. To me speed was not essential – reliability was. For my requirements 'from nought to 30 in 20 seconds' would do. In order to discover the car of my dreams I went to the London Motor Show. Unfortunately, the exhibition was so crowded that other people's backs and some bathing beauties draped over cars' bonnets or roofs was all I could see. Glossy, highly technical brochures did not interest me either. but to look at the same time at a car and a glamour girl just did not make sense to me. So I said to myself: "Max, boy, forget glossy brochures and bathing beauties. Go to a busy road junction and see what sort of car people are buying. If a car is very popular it must be both very good and very reliable."

Having delivered this wise sermon to myself I took a pad of paper and a pencil and went to Hyde Park Corner to carry out my own survey. Among the small family saloons I had in mind three makes were much in evidence: the Volkswagen Beetle, the much-advertised Austin A40 and the Morris Minor. As each of these cars passed by I made a tick in the corresponding column on my paper. In an hour my survey was finished. The Morris Minor scored best. The following day another survey was completed at Marble Arch. The result was the same. Pleased with the outcome I exclaimed with satisfaction: "Hooray, buy British!"

Having chosen the car in such an unromantic way, on Saturday 13 April I went to the sole London distributors, Stewart & Arden at Acton, to see whether I could place an order. Although I was there quite early in the morning a queue had already formed in front of the Sales Office. We all sat on a bench similar to those in old-fashioned surgeries and as each prospective buyer left the Sales Office we would slide along the bench one place nearer to the door. My visit and negotiation with the charming and most efficient salesman, Mr Ridley, was short and very much to the point. There was not much to chose from anyway. I settled for a Morris Minor 1000, two-door saloon, de-luxe version, birch grey with red upholstery. Total costs: £675 6s 3d. When I was asked to pay a deposit I felt hot under the collar. The fact that a deposit might be required had never entered my head and as I did not have my cheque book with me, and not much cash either, I proffered £5.

"Is this enough?" I asked. Much to my relief back came the answer: "Quite enough, Sir". The delivery date remained uncertain. My interview did not last quite ten minutes. Business was certainly brisk. At that rate six cars were sold every hour, while stocks lasted.

At that time H.R.H. Prince Charles had just started to attend the primary school at Knightsbridge.

Three months later a letter arrived advising me that the car was ready for collection. Instructions regarding payment were also enclosed: "preferably cash, or banker's draft". In case of payment by cheque a car would not be released before the cheque was cleared, and in case of a delay, for whatever reason, the car would be allocated to the next person on the list. Hire-purchase transactions were not looked upon with favour. All this seemed to me a very sound business attitude.

By 19 July all formalities were completed and when I came to collect it the car was waiting for me in the adjoining depot. As the milage stood at '75' I enquired whether they had taken the car for a test run. No, they had not, they said. The factory had. As car-transporting lorries did not exist in those days all cars had to be driven to dealers individually; consequently the 75 miles on the clock consisted of the factory test run plus the journey from Oxford to London.

I never gave the car a name. The powers that be have done this by allocating to it the number '79 MMM', the obvious interpretation being 'My Morris Minor', or simply MMM. In recognition of its consistent faithful service I changed its name to *Magnificient Morris Minor* — hence also the title of this book. Everybody else, however, calls it quite correctly: Max's Morris Minor.

The de-luxe version included a heater, in those days a rarity in mass-produced cars, and the front seats were covered with real leather. I was glad that there was a starting handle among the tools. With my very first car in my hands, that night I slept on laurels.

* * *

In order to put the year 1957 into better perspective let it be mentioned that this was the fifth year of Queen Elizabeth's II's reign, while on the other side of the Atlantic the White House in Washington was occupied by the thirtythird USA President, Dwight Eisenhower; the British Prime Minister, Sir Anthony Eden, had just resigned; the world's first spaceship, Sputnik I, was launched into the Earth's orbit; the Rock-and-Roll craze was in full swing and Elvis Presley reigned supreme; Belgium, France, Germany, Holland, Italy and Luxemborg had formed the Common Market; Great Britain abolished the death penalty — with a few exceptions; Agatha Christie's theatre thriller *The Mousetrap* had been running in London for five years – and it is still running; the predecimal £ sterling consisted of twenty shillings – respectively 240 pennies; there was not a single mile of motorway in this country, there was no colour television, no heart transplants, no kidney machines, no MOT (Ministry of Transport) tests, no parking meters, no traffic wardens, no hovercraft, no Concorde, no ocean-going liner QE2, no North Sea Oil, no Berlin Wall, no litres, no metres and no Sunday Colour Supplements.

R 39956

STEWART & ARDERN LTD
Sole London Distributors of Morris Cars and Morris-Commercial Vehicles

MORRIS HOUSE
The VALE. ACTON. W3
AND REGIONAL DEPOTS

ACT.R.39956   9th. July.   19 57

M. Horvat, Esq.,
44, Primrose Gardens,
London.
N.W.3.

	DELIVERY from Acton. DATE S.A.P.	PART EXCHANGE ALLOWANCE	DEPOSIT		
To supplying one Morris Minor 1000 2-door Saloon de luxe, Birch Grey/Red - complete to Manufacturers' catalogue specification.			£433	10	-
To Purchase Tax.			218	2	-
To delivery from Oxford to London.			3	3	-
To supplying and fitting Registration Plates.			2	10	-
To Licence fee from 1st. July to end of year.			6	11	3
To Undersealing Car.			11	10	-
			£675	6	3
Less Deposit.			5	-	-
Balance.			£670	6	3

Reg. No. 79.MMM.   Job No. 4278
Chassis No. FBB13/518355.   Engine No. 80966
Invoice No. 169785.
Mr. Ridley. Acton.
E.&.O.E.
CHASSIS NO...............................   ENGINE NO.........................

11

THE RUNNING-IN PERIOD

According to general belief only 500 miles are required to 'run-in' an engine. After that all working surfaces are supposed to be smooth enough for high speeds. Several years previously, however, I had witnessed the amount of muck and metal particles which came out of another car with its first oil change. This made me decide to give MMM a much longer running-in period. If an engine needed only 500 miles to wear itself in, such an engine, I said, would be worn out by the time it had done 20,000 miles. And I wanted MMM to last much longer than that. Whether this policy would pay any dividends remained to be seen.

During the period of exploring London speeds were slow and there was a lot of gear work. MMM's first long journey was that from London to Land's End. Our route went via Stonehenge. At that time the 'menhirs' were not fenced in. These giant pieces of rock as fat and as tall as Rolls-Royces standing on their ends, stood in the field, quite close to the road, just as they have done for thousands of years. Although easily accessible at any hour of the day or night, they needed no fence, no gate, nothing. During barbaric times they were respected and nobody touched them. Only in modern times, when Tom, Dick and Harry decided to immortalise their visits with inscriptions 'Tom woz here' or the like, or tried to break a piece off to take home as a souvenir, have the authorities found it necessary to protect the 'menhirs' by erecting a fence, installing a gate and appointing sharp-eyed wardens. This, I believe, is what we call Progress of Civilisation.

At Land's End the country, crowned by the 'First and Last House in England', ends in the shape of a massive ridge of turf-topped granite, which defiantly juts out into the sea. Looking at that fine turf one could imagine oneself to be in a garden, but judging by the deafening noise of the Atlantic waves pounding the rocks so mercilessly and incessantly one rather gets the sensation of being on a battlefield. The setting is truly dramatic, almost menacing.

That extremely enjoyable and 880 mile long tour of Devon and Cornwall should not be looked upon as a special achievement because literally thousands of Morris Minors — and other cars — have done it with ease. However, I found it gratifying to be able to state the fact that MMM has visited Land's End, the westernmost point of England.

Having covered a distance of 8,900 miles by the end of 1959 MMM was deemed properly run-in and ready for faster runs. MMM was more than two years old before the first stretch of the M1 was opened to traffic in November 1959. That stretch ran from London to Crick and was only 75 miles long.

A HISTORIC BIRTHDAY

In the early part of 1960 MMM took part in a rather interesting historic event. On Friday 19 February it was announced that the Queen had given birth to a son. The newsreader added that crowds of people were gathering in front of Buckingham Palace cheering the new-born baby. As the weather that evening was very agreeable my family and I hopped into MMM drove to Buckingham Palace and joined the crowd. The occasion was enjoyable and lasted well into the night. I was glad that MMM was also there representing the Morris Minor family. Back at home, and half asleep, I made a quick entry in MMM's logbook: "The Queen gave birth to a baby boy. Mileage: 9,450." A few days later the baby Prince was given the name of Andrew.

*   *   *

JOHN O' GROATS

Ullapool

Inverness

Glenlivet

Balmoral

Fort William

Perth

Glasgow

Edinburgh

SCOTTISH BORDER

Gretna

Newcastle

Ripon

York

Hull

Lincoln

Derby

Stratford-on-Avon

Oxford

London

LAND'S END

MMM GOES TO JOHN O'GROATS

In the course of its life MMM went twice to John O'Groats: the first time in 1960, then again in 1984. On both occasions the itinerary was the same: going north on the east side of the country, and coming back on the west.

In 1984, on the stretch from Inverness to John O'Groats very many people waved to us — some from their windows, others from their gardens or fields. I was puzzled. They did not know us, and we did not know them. Yet the greeting was quite distinct and friendly. Only a day or so later as I sat in the lounge of the John O'Groats hotel it occured to me that all those people were not waving to us personally. They were greeting MMM — the blood relative of the Morris Minor they had once owned and loved, the one which made them happy, and which, in all probability, never let them down, just the same as MMM had never let me down.

* * *

THE JOHN O'GROATS CERTIFICATE

In 1984, prior to departing from John O'Groats, a trophy in the form of a Certificate, decorated with coloured illustrations of the main features of the area, was presented to MMM by Laurie Green. The text read:

> *This is to certify* that *Max Horvat* ('The Old Man') with ('79 MMM') mileage 138,648, has on the 23 day of June, 1984 experienced the achievement of reaching John O'Groats, the scenic landmark in the far north of Scotland. John O'Groats is 876 miles from Land's End — the greatest distance between any two points on the British Mainland.
>
> *Signed:* W. D. Mowat (and) Laurie Green.

That certificate, available from the souvenir shop owner, Mr Mowat, does not cost the earth. The problem is to get to the shop.

MMM GOES TO EUROPE
25 August 1961   Mileage: 17,200

At the beginning of 1961 MMM was three and a half years old, with 14,400 miles on the clock. The prevalent belief among motorists in those days was that such an age and mileage was the limit at which one ought to sell one's car. In this respect my office colleagues were no excepetion and they sold theirs every two years or so. They also did their best to convince me that I would be a fool not to do the same. With one ear I listened to them, and with the other to my engine. Considering that MMM had been run-in carefully, had not been involved in any serious accident and was still running sweetly and economically, surely it was bound to last a bit longer. So I kept it. But before MMM starts to give me trouble it must, I said, take me to Europe.

Summer came soon and on 25 August 1961 MMM was on its way to Europe. Already at Dover I was in the holiday spirit. On my arrival, in the evening, the port was a sea of blazing light. The stage, with the white Cliffs of Dover as the backdrop, was far more impressive than anything I ever saw in a theatre. The car ferry attendants, clearly visible in their immaculate white overalls, made the traffic flow very smoothly. On seeing the AA (Automobile Association) emblem on MMM's radiator grill the AA Patrolman saluted in a friendly way as if to say: "Hello, MMM! Nice to see you go to Europe. Pleasant journey!"

Loading the cars into ships by crane, which I still admired in 1950, ended at Dover in 1951. And in 1961 I was delighted to drive MMM onto the ferry myself.

At that time my brother Rudi worked in West Germany and he decided to join me. At Stuttgart we took the Autobahn towards Munich: this was the stretch on which some years previously the British Motor Corporation had tested their cars. Two Morris Minors were among them. The British Motor Corporation chose the German Autobahn because at that time there were no motorways in England and other open roads were not long enough for such tests.

Those cars were driven at speed up and down the Autobahn for 25,000 miles to find out how they would stand up to such rigours. The runs would start early in the mornings to enable each car to cover a distance of 600 to 800 miles every day. The run Karlsruhe-Stuttgart-Munich and back amounted to 260 miles. On many an occasion such a lap was covered in around four hours.

Sundays were reserved for car servicing and rest. The results were better than expected. The British Motor Corporation had thus obtained conclusive proof that Morris Minors would satisfactorily stand up to a treatment as rough as they were likely to receive from their owners in the course of three to four years. Naturally, I felt very happy to own such a reliable steed and drive it along that very same stretch.

16

Later on MMM had to swallow a bitter pill in Austria: the Grossglockner Pass. The long and arduous climb began soon after Zell-am-See. At first I tried to keep pace with other cars but Rudi warned me not to.

"Look, brother", he said, "the top of the pass is not only far away, it is very high too. This is going to be a severe test as regards both your car and your driving technique. Now, right here, at the bottom of this 20 mile (32 km) long climb you have to choose a speed which will bring us to the top without trouble."

"How fast? Twenty mph? or perhaps thirty?" I enquired.

"I cannot tell you this, listen to what your engine tells you. Choose your gear and stay in it. This is what native drivers do."

The engine soon made it clear that the hairpin bends were too sharp even for twenty mph. So I changed down into second gear. This proved slow enough for the hairpin bends and fast enough for the straight stretches in between. Running for nearly an hour in second gear this modest and unpretentious little British car reached the top of the 8,430 ft (2,572 m) high pass without difficulty, while several bigger cars had to stop because of overheating. Here it should be borne in mind that the Grossglockner Pass is higher than the Simplon, Great St Bernard and St Gotthard Passes.

For the descent Rudi quoted another golden rule: "Going downhill always engage the gear you would use going up hill, and stay in it. And do not use the brakes."

MMM's first visit to Europe was a great success. The tour amounted to 2,170 miles (3,470 km) with a petrol consumption of 51 mpg and no technical trouble.

Later, whenever MMM went to Europe — and it went year after year, sometimes even twice a year — the Grossglockner experience has been the guiding light on all alpine road climbs.

Several continental itineraries were nearly identical. At first Dover was the most useful Channel port, and with regard to roads the German Autobahns were favourite. However, with the improvement in the road system, particularly in France, and with the cross-Channel ferry services starting to operate from the south coast, the Newhaven-Dieppe crossing proved more convenient.

The European tours varied in character too. On some of them MMM was the main protagonist doing all the hard climbing and running around while its passengers were privileged to sit in comfort and watch the rest of the world go by. On other occasions MMM's task was to go from A to B. There it would deposit its passengers to let them do their bit on foot, by canoe or whatever, and then bring them home.

It would be beyond the scope of this book to give detailed descriptions of all journeys. That is why they are only enumerated in Part 3.

MMM's 10th ANNIVERSARY

July 19 1967 was a great day in MMM's life: its tenth birthday anniversary, with the clock standing at 51,000 miles. Such mileage may seem rather small, but as most of it was done in and around London, all without mechanical trouble, MMM's performance during these ten years could not be called anything but fabulous. The decision not to dispose of MMM as suggested by my office colleagues in 1961 has paid dividends, very handsome dividends indeed.

*   *   *

Soon after MMM's tenth anniversary I had to give up my job because my employers had moved out of London. The idea of a change did not appeal to me, but luckily there was a pleasing aspect to my new work: it involved foreign languages, several of them.

A year prior to changing my job I became a member of the Swiss Alpine Club, section Interlaken, which ought to be useful from the linguistic point of view. Although the Swiss have no language of their own, they have, in fact, four official languages: French, which is spoken in the regions bordering on France; Italian and Romansh, in the areas near Italy; and German in those parts close to Germany and Austria. From my point of view Switzerland was an ideal territory both as regards mountaineering and language practice. Naturally, I was eager to take advantage of every opportunity to hop across the Channel.

MMM IS WORTH ONLY £25

In 1973 I was seized by the desire to trade-in MMM for something slightly faster and more up-to-date. Although it was sixteen years old I expected to obtain a reasonable price owing to its excellent state of preservation. The first dealer I approached looked up his copy of *Glass's Guide* – that little book giving current market value of secondhand cars. All he offered was £25. Highly displeased with the price I went to another dealer. "What? ... a Morris Minor? No, no, thanks ... no Morris Minors" and he turned his back on me. The third dealer, rather interested, examined MMM closely, then without referring to *Glass's Guide* but with a magnanimous gesture also offered £25. "Only good for spare parts", was his verdict. Knowing that nothing was wrong with MMM, I, feeling both injured and insulted, decided once more to hang on to it for a bit longer.

At that time a 3,000 mile service cost £13. In my view only a fool would pay so much to get serviced a car which is worth so little. A compromise had to be found. "As I have to put up with MMM", I said to myself, "MMM will have to put up with me servicing it." After all, I felt fairly confident in this respect because in the past I had attended evening classes for car maintenance. And true enough, with the help from the manual and some friends there was little I could not do myself. Judging by its performance MMM was quite happy with the service it received from me.

MMM's 'LAST' EUROPEAN TOUR

MMM's 20th European journey was excellent. Destination: Switzerland. Because Zermatt is a traffic-free town MMM had to be left on the enormous car park at Täsch and the journey completed by cog railway. The alpine scenery in that region was superb. Not only that. On my arrival the 'gates of heaven' had opened and perfect weather, complete with picturesque clouds in the right places at the right moments, was in constant supply. And there was no wind. Wherever I went conditions were ideal. I was as happy as a lark.

By the time my walks were completed the holiday atmosphere changed at a stroke. The sun vanished, Monte Rosa, Matterhorn and all other 'horns' disappeared in clouds. The ever lower descending fog eradicated the horizon and when MMM's doors were unlocked the 'gates of heaven' were firmly closed. No mountain seemed to exist anywhere near. The only thing visible was fog, fog and more fog. Still, I was very happy because all my wishes had been fulfilled.

On the way home I mused over the last nineteen years during which MMM had taken me twenty times to Europe and always brought me back without trouble. To ask for more, I felt, would be tempting Providence.

As my retirement, not so far off, would put an end to my motoring I believed that this tour was MMM's very last journey in Europe. And twenty seemed a nice figure for MMM's European journeys to end up with.

MMM IS TWENTY YEARS OLD

1977 was the year of the Queen's Silver Jubilee, and on July 19 of that year MMM had reached the age of twenty. Proud of this fact I wrote to Messrs Stewart & Ardern to say how pleased I was with the car which they had sold to me twenty years ago. However, as they had ceased trading my letter landed in the office of their successors, Henlys Ltd. Subsequently, the 6 October was fixed to inspect MMM as a matter of historic interest. On arrival at the Henlys' branch at Barnes, London, MMM was greeted by Henlys' Regional Director, Mr A. W. C. Coleman; by British Leyland's Press Officer, Peter Kingsbury; and by the Barnes' Branch Manager, Mr Phillips. MMM was examined, the original documents produced and MMM's diaries perused. The car's condition and past performance were greatly admired.

After the inspection, Mr Coleman – a businessman from top to toe – suggested that I should trade-in MMM and buy a new Morris Marina. They would allow me, he said, the full amount I paid for the car twenty years ago provided that all documents together with twenty road licensing discs and car diaries were handed over also. That offer was really generous and very tempting, but I declined.

MMM also got from Mr Coleman a prize in the form of four gallons of petrol. Very appropriately this was used to visit Lord Nuffield's Birthday Centenary Exhibition at Oxford.

Later I was perplexed as to MMM's trade-in value. One day it was £25, next time £675. But Henlys certainly knew what they were talking about.

A few months later an article about MMM appeared in one of British Leyland's newsletters.

PARTNER FOR SPAIN WANTED

1 October 1979   Mileage: 113,360

With no more European journeys on my mind MMM was used for a great number of shorter runs on home territory — particularly when a succession of overseas friends and relatives descended upon me in 1978. They all were, in turn, taken to dozens of stately homes and castles which they greatly admired, and they were also highly impressed by MMM's impeccable performance.

With my retirement in January 1979 the door to my complete freedom opened fully, but somehow there seemed to exist a vacuum. I felt a fervent wish to make only one more visit to Europe, definitely the last one. By day and night I dreamt of a long, long journey somewhere in the sun. In the end my dreams crystallised into a decision to make a circular tour of Spain with a longer stay at Almunecar, a small place in that 'tropical corner of Europe' near Malaga. For such a venture only two accessories were required: first, a reliable car, which I had, and second, a suitable partner, which I had not.

However, on hearing that I was looking for a companion my young neighbour, Laurie Green, nearly fifty years my junior, was quite enthusiastic about coming with me, but with his two-weeks' holiday entitlement there was no hope. I needed a partner for two months.

Laurie worked for a public authority and applied for unpaid leave. As it so often happens, he was turned down with a clear-cut "No". Displeased with such an outcome he went a step further and lodged an appeal with his top boss. However, as the sacred duty of top bosses is to uphold decisions of departmental heads that interim "No" became a final "No".

In order to discover a partner somehow somewhere I went down the list of all my friends and acquaintances, right from A to Z, but to no avail. "Sorry, I cannot" was the staple answer I received from people I had approached. As time kept passing by my heart kept sinking and just as I was on the verge of giving up my plans Laurie came to see me.

"I have resigned, and I am coming with you", he said.

"Resigned? You must be mad. To give up a perfectly good job while the number of unemployed is above one million?" said I.

"I wish to widen my horizon and when I am back I feel confident I shall not join that million. Seek ... and ye shall find", said he.

I admired him for his courage and was glad to go to Spain in the company of such a man. Our plan was to see the land and its people without spending much time in towns. Our tent was going to be our castle. On 1 October 1979 we were off.

22

Our prospective long stay in the 'tropical corner of Europe' did not quite materialise owing to the heaviest rains in living memory, but otherwise our journey, down to the last inch, went exactly as planned. Even better. On Guy Fawkes' Day our sunbathing session at Cordoba was unexpected and unique. The map shows our route.

A few days after our return home Laurie was offered his old post back. He politely declined that offer because he had already secured a post elsewhere, and a better one at that!

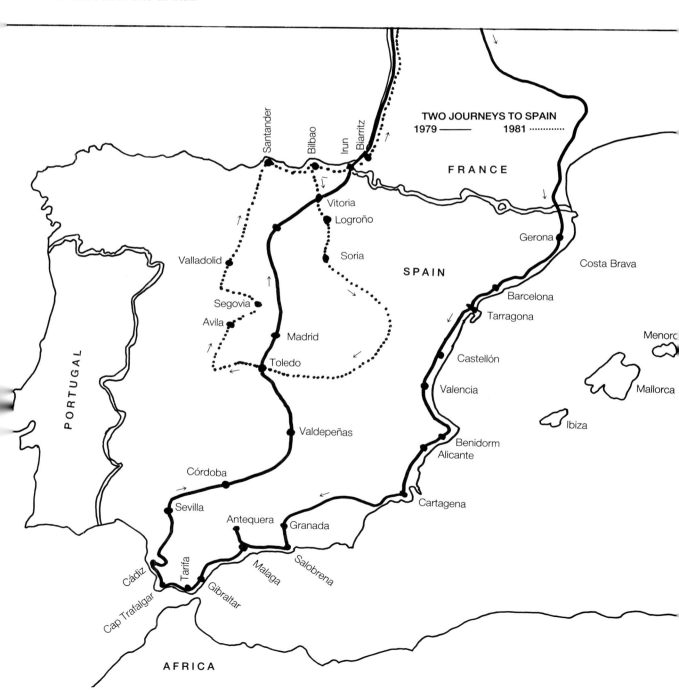

TWO JOURNEYS TO SPAIN
1979 ——— 1981 ············

MMM GOES TO ROME
1 September 1981   Mileage: 126,300

During the Spanish tour in 1979 it was a pleasant surprise for me to find that neither MMM nor I were too old for long European journeys. So, in 1980, I went abroad twice. First, in spring, to Switzerland with Laurie and Carol. All went well then. But the second tour, in autumn, was remarkable because it was the strangest as regards planning, destination and company. Nothing, absolutely nothing, went as originally planned. Hence a detailed description.

Rovert, who lived round the corner, was known to me for more than a year. He was an interesting, well-mannered character, around thirty years of age, and unemployed. On one occasion he assisted me in my garden and it was then that I learned that he was a university graduate, had travelled a lot and had even done some mountaineering in the Himalayas. The only thing I did not like about him was that he was a squatter. Still, he appeared acceptable as a partner for two weeks in Switzerland.

Our target was the Jungfrau in the Bernese Oberland, but by a strange coincidence we landed at Saas Fee, in the Pennine Alps. By another strange coincidence, on the third day there, he injured his leg so badly that he could not walk. And he said "Goodbye" to me. However, the strangest thing of all was my discovery that he was a drug addict. Our partnership, while it lasted, was quite pleasant.

With Rovert gone I was left high and dry. The only friend I could rely on was the levelheaded and most obedient MMM.

Lonely and dispirited, I went just for a day to the Simplon Pass, but before starting the journey home I rang some friends in Bologna just to say "hello". On hearing where I was Professor Greci invited me to visit them. "Bologna is only three to four hours driving away. You must come."

Bologna? ... To go, or not to go? ... I went.

The road going via Domodossola, Lake Maggiore and Milano was fast. MMM liked it. Bologna, a university town since 1200 AD, had much to offer to visitors: a fine cathedral, two leaning towers, twenty miles of arcaded streets, medieval architecture plus Sasso Marconi – the place from which the first message was sent out by radiotelegraphy. At the end of my three-day stay with this charming family I rang some other friends at Livorno to say "hello", just as I did from Simplon. Mrs Carletti, an old acquaintance of mine from the Linguist Club in London, answered the telephone. "You, Max, ... at Bologna? ... Splendid! You must come to see us. It will take you only two to three hours driving to get to Livorno."

Livorno? ... To go, or not to go? ... I went.

So instead of going north my itinerary took me south, farther and farther from home. How would MMM react to this extension?

The autostrada over the Appenine Mountains was teriffic. A series of bends with tunnels and viaducts alternating for miles on end! The ravines were deep, the mountains rough and high and there were no straight streches in the road. Tolls were payable from time to time: £2.50 per 100 miles. Quite acceptable, I felt. However, my stop at the toll booth at Montecatini Terme contained an element of surprise for me: the middle-aged man at the pay counter was totally uninterested in the money I tendered. He just stared at MMM. Then with a shrewd twinkle in his eye said in good English: "I wish to buy your car. Just tell me how much you want for it?" He obviously knew what he was after.

"Sorry, my car is not for sale, at least not yet", said I.

"Your car is a gem ... I worked in England ... I owned one ... they stopped to produce them ten years ago ... and now I would dearly love to buy one."

This, I found, was a great compliment to all Morris Minors, MMM included.

At Pisa MMM made a stop to pay homage to the Leaning Tower, and soon afterwards, at the home of the Carletti family at Livorno, we were refreshing our memories of the good old days in London in the 'fifties. Their visit to England in 1977 was also brought to mind because on that occasion MMM took them one day to Windsor Castle, and on another day to Oxford.

When 'papa' Luigi learned that I had never seen Rome he said that I must go there — particularly since it is *only* three to four hours driving away! As I had already twice extended my journey in the direction away from home, a visit to Rome was out of the question. And that was "definite".

The following day Luigi returned from work with the news that he had booked me in at the Hostel of the Suore della Reparazione in Rome. He also made a plan of all the places I ought to visit. To get to Rome is easy, he said. All I would have to do was follow the superstrada Via Aurelia which runs in a straight line along the west coast of Italy. A superstrada, he explained, is the official classification given to some trunk roads which are not quite as fast as an autostrada, but are nearly as good and there are no tolls to pay.

"Never say 'never' to a sensible suggestion" has been a favourite slogan of mine for a long time. So I bowed to what was ordained by Luigi: Rome ... only three to four hours away!

At Rome Luigi's plan was strictly adhered to and after four delightful days I felt grateful to him for sending me to the Eternal City.

As my intended two weeks in Switzerland turned out to be four weeks in Italy, the 1,000-mile-long journey home would have to be a non-stop affair, said I:

well, a non-stop by my standards.

I dreaded the prospect of travelling alone because a car breakdown with nobody to assist me would be a catastrophe.

The journey home went via Genova and Aosta. To save time and shorten the climb over the pass, the Great St Bernard road tunnel was a splendid alternative. But there, halfway up, lay a heavy lorry, overturned, right across the road. The accident must have happened minutes before my arrival. Had I been there earlier, in its path, MMM would have been a write-off. And, probably, so would I. My non-stop journey was thus interrupted for quite a while. The tunnel toll amounted to 9,400 Lire, or in round figures £5.

The weather and scenery on the Swiss side were glorious. At Martigny I felt that I was already on home ground. That day's run included more than three hours in second gear, on and off. Some autumnal fog delayed progress also with the result that my non-stop journey home lasted full four days, good night rests included. The motorway 'peage' in France was 2½ pence a mile, the same as in Italy.

This strange month-long journey amounted to 2,415 miles (3,860 km). It seemed a real odyssey to me, who, at that time, was approaching my seventieth birthday.

MMM lived up to its reputation: no trouble. A real gem!

As if by a miracle not a drop of rain fell from the day MMM left London to the moment it came back. This, indeed, was MMM's strangest journey.

MORRIS MINOR OWNERS CLUB

During the twentythree years of its production, and afterwards, the small, friendly and reliable Morris Minor has given great satisfaction to millions of drivers and their passengers. Although it has never been a prestige car, many a British heart was saddened by learning that its manufacture had ceased. At first it did not seem to matter but soon spare parts were in short supply. The number of Morris Minor dealers had diminished too. Many Minor owners felt at a loss. There was no focal point to go to.

Then in 1976, the enthusiastic Minor owner, Tom Newton, of Scunthorpe, and two friends of his formed the Morris Minor Owners Club. Steve Coupland became the chairman, Tom himself the secretary and Mick Coupland the treasurer. The response to advertisements for members was so encouraging that already in April 1977 a rally was held at Stanford Hall. Twentyeight Minors from various parts of the country appeared on the scene ... a humble but propitious beginning. That day the first annual general meeting took place too. The committee was enlarged by Derek Porter as newsletter editor, and Pat Wilson as spares secretary. Towards the end of 1978 the membership rose to the 400 mark.

Later, with John Frye as chairman and first Paul Davies and then Ray Newell as secretaries, the Club's development got into full swing: branches were established, a spares service and an insurance scheme were organised and Club regalia was introduced.

Naturally the media became interested in the Club too. Paul Davies was interviewed by Frank Bough at Pebble Mill, members' cars were provided for TV commercials and for television's *Sorry* starring Ronnie Corbett. Many articles soon appeared in the national press about the 'cult car' which until recently was referred to only as a vehicle for the transport of vicars and district nurses. Owing to media publicity the number of members by the end of 1980 rose to 3,400. Since then the Club has gone from strength to strength. In January 1981 it was given limited company status and its commercial aspects were dropped. The name remained the same. Only the letters LTD were added to it.

Club events, in the form of show rallies organised on a local, regional and national basis, became regular features. The National Rally, celebrating the Club's Tenth Anniversary, at Weston Park, Shropshire, in 1986, attracted 1,400 Minors. As these lines are written the Club has 47 branches up and down the country and its membership is in excess of 12,000.

After 1980 the Club also started to compete in the budding Classic Car Shows with great success. It kept winning awards for immaculately preserved cars as well as for its splendid display stands. The Club's original broadsheet newsletter became a bi-monthly magazine called *Minor Matters*; and ever since it has been a valuable source of information for car restoration, maintenance, spare parts and social events. From 1980 onwards the Club became a significant factor in MMM's life too because I have also become a member.

In 1983 the Club arranged its first visit to Europe. This was an inexpensive 60-hour excursion to Fontainebleau, just south of Paris. It was a great success. More than 100 cars took part. Many a timid driver who would not venture to go to Europe on his own, learned on that occasion that there was no problem with driving on the wrong side of the road. There was plenty of hilarity, particularly when groups of Minors, aiming at the same target, met travelling in opposite directions.

After Fontainebleau there was a MOT (Minor Overseas Tour) every year. So far Alkmaar in Holland, Interlaken in Switzerland, Ribeauvillé in Alsace/France, St Rémy-de-Provence also in France, Diekirch in Luxemburg, and La Colle-sur-Loup, again in France, have all been visited in turn. MMM went to Europe with the Club three times and every single tour was a resplendent success in brilliant weather. On these tours the number of participating Minors was always above the one hundred mark. In 1990 the Club visited Amboise in the Loire Valley, France.

Morris Minor Owners Clubs also exist in Australia, Denmark, France, Holland, Norway, New Zealand and Switzerland. In USA the club's names are: Morris Minor Registry and Morris Owners Association of California. In this country there are also independent clubs with the same scope, i.e. North East Morris Minor Club at Peterlee, Co Durham, and Cornwall Morris 1000 Club at Truro, Cornwall.

SOME TECHNICAL DETAILS

All through its life MMM was serviced in accordance with the manufacturer's instructions. But even so some components had to be replaced owing to wear and tear, corrosion, deterioration caused by passage of time or accidental damage. Naturally MMM had received its share of dents and scratches, but the repairs were always so easy that within a matter of hours MMM would be on its way again.

On European tours tyre pressure, level of engine oil, and water in the battery and radiator were checked daily first thing in the morning. On some tours in hot weather the amount of distilled water needed for the battery was much greater than the amount of oil needed for the engine. To complete a long tour without attending to the battery would spell the battery's doom. And 1,000 miles servicings were carried out whenever they fell due irrespective of whether the locality was a motorway, an alpine road or a campsite.

Here is a list of components, in alphabetical order, showing how often they were replaced during the thirtythree years covering a distance of 165,000 miles:

Battery   Six times. They, all reputable brands, lasted anything between four and seven years. On the few occasions, particularly in winter, when a battery was flat a swing with the starting handle always brought the engine to life immediately. Not in vain is the Morris Minor called 'reliable'.

Brake shoes & cylinders   These were replaced twice, the master cylinder once.

Carburettor   After fifteen years and 81,000 miles a new carburettor of the 1100-type was fitted. This proved advantageous because it has increased engine power.

Clutch   MMM is now on its third clutch. The original one lasted 82,700 miles. The second lasted only 58,000 miles although the spare parts had been genuine and the gearchanging technique the same as before. It is just the traffic jams which are now longer and more frequent.

Distributor   After 83,000 miles a new distributor of the 1100-type was fitted owing to an unidentifiable fault. This change also proved advantageous because it eliminated the 'kick-back' which was particularly unpleasant when the starting handle was used. And in winter it was used regularly in order to spare the battery.

Dynamo   After twentyfive years and 131,000 miles the original Lucas dynamo seemed a bit noisy and worn out. When it was taken out to be exchanged for a factory rebuilt unit the date of manufacture, 'June 1957', stamped on its casing, came to light. To me this was an interesting detail worthwhile preserving. So rather than exchanging it, the dynamo was taken to the Lucas Service Department in North London for an overhaul. There, at the service counter, I, full of pride, pointed out the dynamo's age. The elderly assistant pushed his eyeglasses down his nose and looked at me silently for a moment. "Only twentyfive years old? The other day we overhauled one of our dynamos which was fortyfour years old", he said and smiled. So, all you Morris Minor owners with dynamos not older than fortyfour years, be at ease!

Exhaust   The original one lasted eleven years, the replacement fourteen years. The third, the present one, is still in a good condition. None of them was in stainless steel, but the mud and dust was occasionally washed off — which helped.

Fan belts   Two fan belts were replaced during servicing when they were found to be cracked. The other two broke while MMM was on a journey: one in the Swiss Alps, the other in the centre of London. The spare belts, from MMM's boot, never took longer than ten minutes to fit. On both occasions this was a simple do-it-yourself job.

Jacking-up brackets   One broke off after thirty years, the other one after thirtyone years. To have new ones welded on by a Morris Garage was in each case a simple and inexpensive job.

Mudguards   Two were replaced; one front, one rear, of which the latter was again a do-it-yourself job costing £2.50 in 1972.

Petrol pump   After fifteen years and 78,000 miles AA assistance was requested for the first time. In the outskirts of London the engine died without warning. But, help came quickly. Diagnosis: worn points. These were cleaned by the patrolman and MMM was on its way again. Delay: forty minutes. Later on, at home, the petrol pump was replaced. The very same thing happened in 1989. Those were the only two occasions when AA help had been invoked.

Radiator   After twentynine years the radiator had 'furred-up' to such an extent that the engine kept overheating. Remedy: a reconditioned radiator.

Regulator (Control Box)   When the battery-charging process became erratic suspicion fell on the sixteen-year-old regulator. The investment of £2 for a new regulator paid ample dividends.

Shock absorbers   After sixteen years both front shock absorbers were worn out and had to be replaced.

Speedometer cable   The original one was replaced after three years owing to a kink, and the replacement had to be renewed twenty years later owing to ordinary wear.

Tyres   MMM is now on its fourth set of tyres. All of them were crossply. Some had to be replaced before their time because they were cut by glass and the damage was beyond repair.

Engine valves & springs   All eight valves and springs were replaced when, after twentyfour years and 129,000 miles the engine was rebored.

Water pump   Replaced three times owing to wear.

Gearbox, propshaft & rear-axle   Have not yet been touched.

Wheel bearings   The wheel bearings, so far, have well stood up to wear. Given 880 wheel rotations per mile, MMM's wheels had up to the end of February 1990, spun round 144 million times!

*   *   *

Some of the splendid places and magnificent scenery which MMM had encountered on its peregrinations at home and abroad are shown on the following pages. As a chronological description of events would render the story in a rather disjointed way, an arrangement, subjectwise more coherent, is aimed at.

MMM ON THE SUSSEX COAST (Many visits)

Being based in London, MMM has visited the South Coast every year, usually several times, always discovering something new.

On the glorious Sussex coast the Seven Sisters, rising perpendicularly into the air and reaching a height of 260 ft (80 m) tower proudly above the sea between Eastbourne and Brighton. In the neighbouring county of Kent the once prosperous seaport of Sandwich lies nowadays two miles inland owing to the sea receding. And in Sussex so does Rye. In the case of the Seven Sisters, however, the situation is reversed. Exposed to the destructive forces of wind, rain and frost, battered and eroded by the waves, the face of the cliffs keeps crumbling and the sea advancing at the alarming rate of 2 ft a year.

The historic battle of Hastings in 1066 which resulted in the Norman conquest of England and initiated far-reaching and lasting changes in English life and language, was fought at a spot slightly to the east of the Seven Sisters. The history of the Sussex coast would not be complete without mentioning the traffic which brought first-class goods into the country from France by the 'gentlemen of the night'. The Birling Gap and the estuary of the Cuckmere were the arteries through which the smugglers filtered their most welcome wares deep into the hinterland.

It was on the run to the Sussex coast on 28 September 1975 that MMM clocked its 100,000th mile.

MMM MEETS A PENNY-FARTHING

3 March 1984   Mileage: 137,300

MMM has met a Penny-Farthing on many an occasion.

The earliest two-wheelers came from France some 200 years ago, but they were crude and heavy contraptions made of wood, without pedals, pushed forward by riders' feet. They were mere 'toys for the adults'. However, the first all-metal bicycle, 'The Ordinary', later called the Penny-Farthing, proved to be a useful means of transport. Its huge front wheel, up to five feet in diameter, enabled the rider to cover a distance of sixteen feet (nearly five metres) with a single turn of the pedals.

Penny-Farthings were also the first bicycles fitted with solid rubber tyres which made speeds of up to 25 miles (40 km) per hour possible. Very fashionable in the 1880s, they cost £18 apiece, which was a lot of money in those bygone days. While the roof of the Morris Minor, as can be seen, is level with the bike's handlebar and saddle, the rider's head rises to eight feet above ground.

There were some 5,000 high-wheelers and more than 200 clubs in existence up and down the country. Many clubs had their own uniform — serge jacket, knickerbockers and pill-box cap. To give the signal 'mount', 'slacken speed' or 'dismount', club captains would often use a bugle. Unfortunately, Penny-Farthings were not safe. A brick or similar object would bring the rider crashing to the ground, head first. Later models of bicyles with pneumatic tyres and a driving chain drove Penny-Farthings out of fashion.

It was heartwarming to see last century's 'King of the Road' rubbing shoulders with MMM.

34

MMM MEETS A VETERAN
2 November 1986   Mileage: 149,680

At the time when steam-driven tractors were the only self-propelled vehicles on the roads, the Locomotive Act of 1865 imposed a speed limit of a maximum 4 mph on open roads and 2 mph in built-up areas. In addition these vehicles had to be preceded by a man on foot carrying a red flag to warn people of the approaching danger. When cars appeared on the roads the same rules applied to them. Dissatisfied with such restriction the motoring fraternity tended to ignore the law. However, offenders could face heavy fines, and, since policemen on bicycles could catch up with 'automobiles', an escape was never easy. Soon the law was changed, the speed limit was increased to the 'dizzy heights of 12 mph', and the red flag was abandoned. To celebrate this achievement the motoring enthusiasts arranged a mass car run from the Metropole Hotel in London to the Metropole Hotel in Brighton. This was in November, 1896. The Veteran Car Club of GB stages every year such a run in which only pre-1904 'crocks' may take part. This most spectacular and most amusing car run in the world takes place on the first Sunday in November, starting, as the rules say, 'from Hyde Park Corner, London, at the grey, grey hour of 8 in the morning'. The picture opposite shows MMM and 'a Veteran' which took part in the London to Brighton run in 1986. This is an Oldsmobile, manufactured in 1903; it has no steering wheel but only a little tiller and its wheels are made of wood. While MMM has four cylinders (948cc) the veteran has only one of 1560 cubic capacity.

37

MMM MEETS A GOLDEN EAGLE
2 July 1984   Mileage: 139,470

Leighton Hall, a manor of great charm near Carnforth, Lancashire, has for centuries been the seat of the Gillow family, the famous furniture manufacturers of Lancaster. On MMM's arrival at Leighton Hall a sweet smile of satisfaction covered the face of the lady of the house, Mrs Susan Gillow-Reynolds. "You know", she said, "my first car was a Morris Minor. I loved it. And I still love them." When she took MMM for a spin that short sharp smack on the gear lever necessary to engage the reverse revealed the fact that an expert Morris Minor driver was at the steering wheel.

In the Middle Ages a proportion of the meat required at Leighton Hall was supplied by trained birds of prey, the descendants of which, reintroduced in 1977, were a great attraction. Eagles, falcons, buzzards, kestrels and owls performed daily in front of an audience seated on the enormous lawn in front of the Hall. Some birds would catch objects thrown into the air, while others would chase in circles a small ball swung on a piece of string. The small ones would fly around and, to the enormous delight of everybody, land on people's heads. The most impressive performer, of course, was a Golden Eagle. Taken by car to the top of a nearby hill and released, he would soar into the air, glide in circles above people's heads, then suddenly go into a steep dive and, with a flypast close to the front row of the audience, land on the handler's outstretched arm: a stupendous sight! At the end of the performance the occasion was captured by photo — Max holding the Golden Eagle.

MMM MEETS A HIGHLAND BULL
26 June 1984   Mileage: 138,900

The world knew of Highland Cattle long ago. The ancient Phoenicians are said to have sailed all the way from North Africa to Scotland to buy the thick hides which they required for the manufacture of their shields.

At Torridon, on the West Coast of Scotland, a nice, short-legged, very shaggy and befringed Highland cow was spotted grazing peacefully. With the farmer's permission MMM was driven into the field for a photograph or two. The cow's horns, each as long as a man's arm, looked terrifying, but since they pointed sideways, in exactly opposite directions, one would think that they were a decoration rather than an instrument for fighting. All went well until a thunder of galloping feet made it clear that danger was coming. A black Highland bull appeared on the scene heading for us — the intruders. In a flash MMM was abandoned and the gate was closed. True, the thin wire fence would be no obstacle for him but very obligingly he stopped. His horns, short and strong, exquisitely curved, tapered to a fine point and both pointing forward like two spears, were obviously designed for one purpose only ... elimination of the enemy. And there he stood, motionless, making sure that his ladies were left alone. The distance between the car, the bull and the gate was far too close for comfort, so the only way to extricate MMM was to trick the potential enemy. While the bull was being distracted by some salty biscuits thrown to him MMM went roaring through the gate, the driver perspiring and breathing heavily like the bull himself.

40

MMM AT ABBOTSFORD
4 June 1960   Mileage: 10,820
18 June 1984   Mileage: 138,215

A huge demarkation rock on the Anglo-Scottish Border at Carter Bar, with 'Scotland' in big letters, indicates to the traveller coming from the south, the exact spot where England ends and Scotland begins. Carter Bar (1,370 ft / 418 m), a formidable pass over the Cheviots, offers wide open views but without a single field, meadow or house in sight for miles around. However, thirty miles further on, halfway between Melrose and Galashiels, stands Abbotsford, the home of the literary giant, Sir Walter Scott. He turned out to be the champion of the Highlands by elevating the clans back to their previous importance and honour, and by giving the kilt again an aura of its previous romantic and aristocratic significance and glory. It was also he who chose the name and spot for his superb multi-turreted mansion, built in the grand Scottish baronial style.

There, the garden walls are adorned with sculptures, old coats-of-arms and inscriptions in stone, some of which Sir Walter found lying on a rubbish heap in Edinburgh. Realising the usefulness of such rubbish he did not hesitate to confirm by deed that "one man's waste is another man's fortune". How clever!

Abbotsford is open to the public and Sir Walter Scott's study, with his writing desk made of wood from one of the ships of the Spanish Armada, looks today exactly as it did when he was alive. The place, teaming with history and cared for with love, is the home of Mrs Patricia Maxwell-Scott, who is a forth-generation descendant of Sir Walter.

MMM AT BRAEMAR CASTLE
6 June 1960   Mileage: 11,142
20 June 1984   Mileage: 138,375

From Cairnwell Pass (2,199 ft/670 m), where patches of snow within arm's reach in June are nothing out of the ordinary, a pleasant descent along the crystal-clear river Clunie Water brought MMM to the leafy, attractive and hospitable village of Braemar. Being completely free from any kind of industrial pollution and situated at 1,100 ft (335 m) above sea level it is an ideal holiday spot. On the first Saturday in September of every year thousands of Scots, men and women, from all over the world gather there to see or take part in the famous Highland Gathering, featuring competitions in Scottish Dancing, pipe playing and the typically Scottish athletics: tossing the caber, throwing the hammer and putting the shot. With nearly everybody wearing the colourful Highland Dress these week-long championships are truly delightful.

A short distance from the village stands Braemar Castle, silent and defiant. This turreted stronghold had a stormy past. Built in 1628 by the Earl of Mar, Regent of Scotland, it was burnt down during the Jacobite fighting. After the Rebellion it was rebuilt to garrison the Hanoverian troops. When it was no longer needed for this purpose it was converted into a private residence of great character. It belongs to Captain A. C. Farquharson of Invercauld, and it is open to the public. Picturesque round towers, narrow spiral staircases, barrel-vaulted ceilings and a star-shaped defensive wall on the outside, are features to please the eye of any visitor and to remain firmly impressed on his mind for a long time.

MMM AT BALMORAL
7 June 1960   Mileage: 11,150
21 June 1984   Mileage: 138,380

Less than ten miles east of Braemar stands another magnificent castle, Balmoral. It is well protected by a river on one side and by a high mountain on the other. The vegetation in the valley of the Scottish river Dee has always had the reputation of being luxuriant and the climate so good that already in 1484 the locality was known under the name of Bouchmoral. Queen Victoria and Prince Albert had visited Scotland several times and took to it. From their physician, Sir Robert Clark, they learned of the advantages of Balmoral. Hence, when its owner, Sir Robert Gordon, died, Prince Albert bought the estate — without even seeing it beforehand! Too small for royal requirments, the old mansion was pulled down and the present-day fairy-tale castle erected. After the Rebellion the political situation in Scotland was far from happy, but the fact that Queen Victoria had chosen a place in the heart of Scotland for her holidays, has contributed more to a true pacification of the Highlands than the bayonets stationed there previously. Ever since 1855 Balmoral has served as a holiday home for the Royal Family.

To be admitted into the castle grounds was indeed an honour for MMM and for Morris Minors in general. A special permit was necessary, of course.

In 1984 MMM was at Balmoral on 21 June, exactly the day of little Prince William's second birthday.

MMM AT THE SCONE PALACE
19 June 1984   Mileage: 138,324

Two miles north of Perth stands Scone Palace, the proud place where the famous Coronation Stone had been kept for some 500 years. This was also the place where, long ago, Macbeth, King of the Scots, was slain. Once upon a time Scone was also a royal residence and the capital of the Kingdom of the Picts. It was there that Scottish Kings were crowned for centuries. The last coronation on Scottish soil took place in 1651 when King Charles II was crowned in a small church on Moot Hill, adjacent to Scone Palace.

The palace's dark and rather austere exterior is in contradiction with the magnificence of its interior. One of its past owners, the First Earl of Mansfield, was Lord Chief Justice for England for thirtytwo years and it was he who passed the historic decision that "any slave who sets his foot on British soil must become a free man." At that time many people were shocked on hearing this, but his word remained law. The palace, full of fine paintings, porcelain and furniture, has been the home of the Mansfields for nearly 400 years.

A very impressive statue of Lord Mansfield, with a Roll in his left hand, stands in St Vincent's Hall of the Houses of Parliament, third on the left.

MMM AT JOHN O'GROATS
8 June 1960   Mileage: 11,320
23 June 1984   Mileage: 138,648

Some 500 years ago the Orkney Islands, the nearest only six miles off the coast of Scotland, belonged to Denmark. When they came under Scottish rule King James IV invited three young Dutch brothers, De Groot, to operate a ferry to the Orkneys. This they did and before long there were eight separate families. During one of their annual gatherings a bitter quarrel broke out about seniority and presiding at the table. To solve the problem old John built himself a house near the harbour. The dining room was octagonal, it had an octagonal table and eight separate doors. Thus at the next gathering the head of each family was able to enter the room through his own door and say that his was the seat of honour. The solution was ideal, and John O'Groats became the name of the hamlet and its surroundings. A truly inhospitable climate and complete absence of vegetation have been a colossal deterrent to prospective settlers. This is why John O'Groats and the thirty square miles around it have a population of around 200. Old John's house has been rebuilt and now it serves as an hotel. The distance from London is 705 miles (1,130 km) and from Land's End 876 miles (1,400 km). Thousands of sportsmen of all calibres go to John O'Groats; some for serious competitions, others for their 'End to End' exploits, or just for fun. Like MMM, they do not stay there. They just come and go.

The bottom picture shows Port Nancon, on the north coast, not far from Bettyhill. The grey area beyond Port Nancon is an island shrouded in genuine Scottish fog and rain.

50

MMM ON THE WHISKY TRAIL
22 June 1984   Mileage: 138,460

To make a 'Grand Tour of Scotland' without visiting a distillery would, in the eyes of a Scotsman, be a cardinal sin, and that was why so many roads are signposted 'Whisky Trail'. A hilly road, classed as 'not suitable for coaches', took MMM from Balmoral to Glenlivet. On this stretch MMM literally jumped over that charming hump-back bridge and near Glenlivet a roadsign made quite, quite sure that nobody missed the distillery.

In the Visitors' Centre an exquisite atmosphere was created by a lifesize replica of a small, secret Highland distillery of long ago. It resembled the Crib, but instead of the usual figures there was the crofter and his family. The fire under the still was the equivalent of the Star. The sheep were represented by two gundogs and a hunter in Highland dress seemed a substitute for the shepherds. His gun stood next to him and at his feet lay a fine specimen of a stag just killed. With a glass of whisky in the hunter's hand and a happy expression on everybody's face the scene looked most genuine. With such introduction the tour of the distillery was most enjoyable. A small charge seemed perfectly justifiable since they let you sample some of their product to feel for yourself how it warms the 'cockles of your heart'.

MMM AT THE LONG JOHN DISTILLERY
22 June 1984   Mileage: 138,475

A rather strange feature which never fails to attract the attention of visitors at the Glenlivet Distillery is a huge pair of weighing scales, with a big wooden barrel in the air on one side. Surely they do not sell whisky by the ton? The situation was quickly clarified for us by a bonnie, kilted and besporraned guide called Finlay. According to him no spirit may be called whisky if it is less than three years old. So whatever they produce must go into storage for maturing. But the amount of whisky in each barrel when it comes out of storage is considerably less than it was when it went in, although nobody has touched the barrels in between. This mysterious loss is called 'The Angels Share'. They are supposed to have taken it. But since buyers would pay only for the actual content of a barrel, in the days gone by whisky was indeed measured in hundredweights and stones instead of in gallons and pints. At Glenlivet MMM's larder was replenished not with a ton of whisky, but just with a number of miniatures.

The road from Glenlivet to Inverness also formed part of the Whisky Trail and as MMM progressed a magnificent housing estate came into view. To find out the secret of why Destiny had placed it right in the middle of nowhere the speed was reduced and MMM found itself in front of the Long John Distillery at Tormore. There, they said, the conditions for establishing a distillery were ideal. And judging by their product they indeed are. At the end of the visit MMM's passenger *and* driver, may God forgive him, left the Long John Distillery with an increased regard for Scotch, the noblest of the noble drinks.

MMM USES SCOTTISH FERRIES

5 June 1960   Mileage: 10,860
13 June 1960   Mileage: 11,780

In 1960 there was no road bridge over the Firth of Forth at Edinburgh. Instead of going a long way round it was simpler to let the Queensferry take MMM across the Firth. As usual, cars were loaded in the order of their arrival.

On the ferry a simple snapshot was taken to record that crossing. Max's family — Slava and Lyerka — are seen standing next to MMM. On the other side of MMM stands a Morris Traveller and a split-screen Minor, while yet another Morris 1000 is behind them. Although they were all loaded in order of their arrival the whole family of Minors was together ... a sign of their extreme popularity ... a lot of them everywhere.

On that occassion, as can be seen, the cars were parked very close to one another. Every square inch of floor space seemed to matter. On another occassion, however, MMM was ferried in style. It had the ferry all to itself. This was the Connell ferry which exists no longer. Of the five ferries MMM used in 1960 only the Kylestrome ferry was still operating in 1984. But there a new road bridge was receiving the finishing touches for the opening by the Queen at the end of August, 1984.

English Channel crossings apart, MMM has also crossed Lake Lucerne twice on the stretch Beckenried-Gersau. And in the south of France a ferry took MMM across the Grand Rhône into the Camargue, and back.

60

MMM CROSSES THE CHANNEL BY AIR

14 June 1969   Mileage: 61,075
29 June 1969   Mileage: 62,400

The glamour of driving one's own car on board a ferry wears a bit thin over the years. By the end of 1968 MMM had crossed the English Channel in both directions nine times by sea and the tenth crossing, in 1969, was done in grand style — by air.

British Air Ferries operated from the airfield at Lydd (Kent), which lies near the coast, halfway between Folkestone and Hastings. To fly a small car and three adult passengers to Le Touquet in France, just slightly south of Boulogne, and back, cost £35 (i.e. only £6 more than going by sea). The airplane, a beefy and noisy Bristol Freighter, would carry four cars and their passengers. Driving the cars on and off the plane was the responsibility of special personnel and in this picture MMM is seen in the process of being loaded. Bookings were, of course, essential but departure times were not given precisely. Four cars could be loaded in ten minutes. So, as soon as cars were to hand, and loaded, the plane would take off. Crossings took some twentyfive minutes and the cruising height was approximately 1,500 ft.

The layout of towns and villages, and the irregular water channels of the marshy coast were fascinating. Much to the regret of many a motorist British Air Ferries have ceased ferrying cars owing to lack of demand during the out-of-season periods.

On this occassion it was somewhat contradictory that MMM had crossed the Channel in the shortest time ever in spite of travelling tail first!

MMM ON THE GROSSGLOCKNER ROAD

30 August 1961   Mileage: 17,960
3 July 1964   Mileage: 33,430

The Austrian mountains, south of Salzburg, called Hohe Tauern form a group of their own, Grossglockner being their highest peak (12,457 ft/3,798 m). MMM has traversed this massif twice: in 1961 from north to south, and in 1964 in the opposite direction. The long approach road, from Bruck, twists its way up and up not along a narrow valley but on the shoulders of mountains offering spectacular views. These change with every inch on every bend with ever-increasing splendour.

The Edelweisspitze is a 'belvedere par excellence' and so is the Fuschertörl. From them a panoramic view can encompass as many as forty snow-capped peaks, all in excess of 10,000 ft. The highest point of the road is 8,435 ft (2,572 m) above sea level. MMM took a solid hour in second gear to get to the top. The bottom photograph taken in the French Alps, shows what alpine roads are like. The Grossglockner road is totally obstructed by snow from late October to late May. The temperature is low even in the best of weathers and, according to that brave character seen in the photograph, shorts should not be worn even for a fiftieth of a second.

Grossglockner and the huge Pasterzen Glacier can best be seen from the Franz-Josef's Höhe, a platform near the idyllic alpine village of Heiligenblut. It may sound macabre to suggest a visit to Heiligenblut's cemetery, but there one can pay respect to the courage of the many who have lost their lives in daring mountaineering attempts. Instead of tombstones on some of the graves there are oversize books with pages made of metal which one can turn and read how many a noble intention ended in disaster.

64

MMM GOES TO ITALY
14 June 1963   Mileage: 26,350

The sense of reliability derived from MMM's impeccable performance during 1962 coupled with the sweet memories of the Grossglockner venture in 1961 were the decisive factors for making another tour in the sunny south of Europe.

In the north-eastern corner of Italy, slightly south of the Brenner Pass, MMM entered a group of mountains called The Dolomites. They differ from the Alps in origin, configuration and character, and like the High Tours in Austria, also form a group of their own. Whilst rivers in this area — Adige, Brenta, Piave and Tagliamento — flow south into the nearby Adriatic Sea, the water immediately across the Italo-Austrian border are carried by a multitude of rivers to the Danube and on into the Black Sea, more than a thousand miles away. Immediately south of the Dolimites Venice entertains her visitors. The Dolomites cover an area so small that they could easily be crossed by car in half a day, be it in the east-west or north-south direction. Small they may be but they contain hundreds of jewels in the form of exquisite mountains, lakes, valleys, passes, high plateaus, flowers, forests, towns and villages. Is there anybody who has not heard of Cortina? It played host to the Winter Olympics in 1956.

The Alps are grandiose and massive, but here the erosion has transformed the primaeval dolomitic mass into mountains, towers and rocks of bizarre shapes indeed. Nowhere can one find so many splendid alpine passes so close together as they are here: Gardena, Rolle, Sella, Pordoi, Campolongo, Falzarego and Tre Croci. They are the principal passes and wherever you go, you cannot go wrong.

MMM IN ITALY AGAIN (CORVARA)
26 June 1964   Mileage: 33,085

During the first walking tour in the Dolomites, in 1963, deep soft snow on a steep slope stopped us in our tracks exactly when the splendid Locatelli Hut — and the stupendous views from it — seemed within easy reach. Brokenhearted, and seeing the weather deteriorate, we vowed that we would come back again. And that was why MMM went again to Italy in 1964.

After descending from the Brenner Pass into Italy for some thirty miles MMM reached the point where the swift mountain stream Gardena meets the even swifter river Isarco. Ponte Gardena is the name of the place where they meet, and this is also the beginning of the marvellous Gardena Valley. It rises consistently towards a pass the name of which, as everbody would guess, is Gardena (7,009 ft/2,137 m). A great spot!

From there MMM wound its way in impressive curves down to Corvara, a sweet alpine village full of native charm. There is plenty of elbow room there for everybody to swing his arms about, to expand his chest and choose a peak, rock-face or ridge on which to test his resources, courage and skill. In summer masses of alpine flora on the slopes along the road greet the visitor on the way to his targets wherever they may be. Outside the village the mighty Sas Songher rises vertically into the air scraping the sky at 8,741 ft (2,665 m).

It was at Corvara that the tent was pitched for a night in unforgettable surroundings.

MMM AT THE RIFUGIO AURONZO

27 June 1964   Mileage: 33,135

After Corvara the next stop was Cortina, in fact Cortina d'Ampezzo to give it its full name. From there a supremely elegant road with grand views of the nearby snow-capped Monte Cristallo (9,958 ft/3,036 m) took MMM over the Tre Croci Pass down to Lago Misurina, an idyllic alpine lake surrounded and sheltered by strangely formed mountains.

During the First World War this area was hotly contested by Austria and Italy. Whoever sat atop the mountains was master of the roads below. Rivers of blood spilled there, however, had one fortunate result: an intricate network of tracks and paths, many of them quite level, have been left behind. Built by soldiers, they once linked trenches and heavy gun emplacements with caverns and observation points cut out of living rock. Now they are a great boon to all those who come there for recreation.

High above Lake Misurina stands Rifugio Auronzo. Named after the nearby peaks once it was a simple mountain hut but now it is a fine hotel. Its altitude of 8,000 ft (2,438 m) with night temperature below freezing point even at the height of summer is no encouragement for camping in its vicinity, although we, MMM included, did so for two nights running, in emergency. The nearby three giant towers of Tre Cime (9,816 ft/2,999 m) offer to the intrepid the severest rock climbs in the world.

When MMM climed that old military road, suitable only for cars with a big ground clearance, it was bottom gear all the way. This photograph, taken from the car park of the Rifugio Auronzo shows the savage Cadini group, with MMM in the foreground – third from the right.

MMM CARRIES CANOES
20 May 1961   Mileage: 15,800
31 May 1974   Mileage: 89,910
4 September 1975   Mileage 98,595

One purpose for which the Morris Minor was not designed was to carry canoes. The very short and curved roof is hardly suitable for roof-racks in general, and long loads in particular. Yet, for those not living near water the temptation to use their Minors as canoe transport is great. As they say 'variety is the spice of life' and this principle applies equally to canoeing scenery. In this respect MMM's fate was no exception. Two roof-bars spaced only 2 ft 6 in (75 cm) apart proved perfectly suitable for carrying canoes up to 17 ft (5 metres) long and up to 60 lb (27 kg) in weight, provided that the canoe was well balanced and properly tied down. The Thames, alongside which MMM had run many a time, is an ideal canoeing ground. Its course, from its source near Gloucester to its entry into the sea at Tilbury near Greenwich, is 210 miles (338 km) long. At the time when railways were not in existence the Thames was a major transport artery. To improve the navigable depth locks were built way back in the seventeen-seventies. Now the non-tidal part of the river could be looked upon as a series of fortyfive lakes separated from one another by a lock.

Many shorter missions apart, MMM took a canoe three times to the furthest navigable point on the Thames, Cricklade; several times to the Norfolk Broads and twice to Switzerland for the purpose of circumnavigating the 50 miles (80 km) long Lake Geneva. Even with crosswinds, speeds up to 35 mph were safe. Indeed, MMM has fulfilled its canoe carrying task admirably.

MMM AND THE SWISS RAILWAYS
20 September 1973   Mileage: 87,340

Following the road from Berne towards Interlaken along the south side of Lake Thun MMM reached the charming market town of Spiez. Built on a promotory, Spiez protrudes far into the lake catching the sunshine from early morning to late evening. Although the eternal snows and ice of the Bernese giants are, as the crow flies, only a dozen miles away (some 20 km), at Spiez and its surroundings there are many miniature vineyards. The sight of vines trailing up house-walls, and bearing ripening grapes, would not be anything out of the ordinary in Italy, but here such an aspect is doubly pleasing.

Without any rivals of comparable size in the proximity the neighbouring, conically shaped Niesen rises to a height of 7,750 ft (2,360 m). It offers glorious views in all directions. Seen from its top the snowcapped Eiger, Mönch and Jungfrau seem to be within arm's reach.

The building engulfed in flowers, shown opposite, is neither a chapel nor a luxury hotel, but the railway station at Mülenen, hardly more than a couple of miles (3 km) from Spiez. From there the cog railway Niesen-Bahn will whisk you up to the top of Niesen in a matter of minutes. Good organisers as they are, the Swiss Railways offered a ticket comprising the return fare, dinner, room and breakfast in a hotel on the top of Niesen for SF40 (approximately £10). This was indeed a most reasonable price for mountaineering in its laziest form. In this alpine paradise around Spiez distances are small: Interlaken is around 10 miles (16 km) away; Adelboden and Kandersteg approximately the same.

MMM IN THE UPPER RHÔNE VALLEY

28 June 1965   Mileage: 39,790
12 September 1980   Mileage: 120,750

The Kanton Walis in the south western corner of Switzerland is reputed for good weather and magnificent scenery. MMM was there half a dozen times, first time in 1965 and last time in 1980.

There, the Swiss part of the Rhône Valley runs, basically from east to west except for a kink at the town of Martigny, and this is the course along which the wild, frothy infant Rhône rushes downhill to pour its water into Lake Geneva. The colossal drop in altitude, some 5,400 ft (1,650 m), indicates that mountains on either side of the river are high. To the north stand the Bernese giants Eiger, Mönch and Jungfrau, to mention only a few, and to the south the Penine Alps, with Monte Rosa, the highest, and Matterhorn, the most formidable in the land. The delightful side valleys: Val d'Entremont — leading to Great St Bernard Pass — Val d'Herens, Val d'Anniviers and Saastal, have all been visited by MMM over the years. At Brig a road branches off for the charming Simplon Pass.

The Rhône valley is windy, but the configuration of the land is such that rainy clouds are taken away. In 1911 the amount of rain in the Sierre area was less than in the Sahara. In the east, where the Rhône Valley ends, the long climbs to the Grimsel and Furka Passes begin. The splendid and easily manageable Susten Pass is also close by. In France MMM has followed the course of the Rhône in the region of Lyon, Avignon and the Camargue. Wines grown on the banks of the Rhône are very popular even among Morris Minor drivers. Hands up, those of you who have not heard of the Côte du Rhône wines.

MMM ON THE FURKA PASS
10 September 1971   Mileage: 74,670
6 September 1976   Mileage: 104,321

In the area south of Lucerne high alpine passes are numerous. The very high and difficult Furka is one of them. My MMM went over it on its thirteenth European journey, and again during its twentieth. The slightly cock-eyed road-sign seen leaning toward MMM proclaims to the world: 'Furka – 2,430 metres, 7,972 ft'. For the convenience of the British who congregated in Switzerland during the Golden Age of Mountaineering, altitudes have been given in feet also. The austere grey building is the Furka Pass Hotel. For the melting snow on its roof it was impossible to say whether it was old or new because on the Furka Pass it never rains. If there is precipitation it is always in the form of snow. There are masses of it and this is why the Furka road is usually closed for eight months a year. A short distance from the top of the pass the road almost touches the Rhône Glacier. This spot cannot be missed. Hotel Belvedere, a big car park and a sign saying 'Gletschergrotte' (Glacier Grotto) are clear indications. From there even ladies in high heels can reach the glacier in one minute! A tunnel driven into the ice, ending in a big ice cave, is a great tourist attraction. The smooth green icewalls, penetrated by daylight, are fascinating and the experience of being in an enormous 'deep freeze' well below the surface of Mother Earth is good value for money.

In the immediate vicinity the exposed layers of broken rock vividly indicate the convulsions Mother Earth had suffered at the time when the Alps were born.

MMM GOES THROUGH THE MONT BLANC TUNNEL
31 August 1971   Mileage: 74,283

The early English travellers going to Italy and wishing to include Paris and Geneva in the intinerary of their Grand Tour would find themselves in a predicament at Geneva. The shortest way into Italy would be via Chamonix (France) and Courmayeur (Italy), but exactly on this stretch rose a most formidable barrier, Eurpoe's highest mountain, Mont Blanc. There it stood solid, huge, frozen, covered with ice, silent and immobile, and with no road over it. However, if only one could reach the banks of the river Dora Baltea on the Italian side of Mont Blanc, barely ten miles from Chamonix as the crow flies, the way into the plain of Lombardy could not be simpler. All one would have to do is follow that river.

One solution open to travellers was to go round via Great St Bernard Pass, by no means an easy feat. The other solution, a detour going south, was even worse. The vision of an easy journey by piercing and going through that frozen giant must have been percolating in the heads of travellers and road builders for a long time. Eventually that dream became reality. In 1965 the 7 miles (11 km) long Mont Blanc Tunnel was opened to traffic. Its construction took six years. Unbelievable as it may sound, at one point the tunnel runs 11,200 ft (3,400 m) below the summit. One end of the tunnel is French, the other Italian.

On its thirteenth European journey MMM entered Italy with ease by going through the tunnel. The photograph opposite shows the Italian side of Mont Blanc with the Brenva Glacier.

MMM AT GIBRALTAR
30 October 1979   Mileage: 115,200

To chase the winter sun is a nice occupation for a millionaire, yet for a pensioner with a car and a bit of initiative this should be no problem either. And exactly such a fate befell the twentytwo-year-old MMM in 1979. With a genuine 113,350 miles on its clock, with camping equipment and two people on board MMM worked its way through France, entered Spain at the eastern end of the Pyrenees and proceeded along the Mediterranean Coast, stopping at many seaside resorts. Soon after Malaga MMM landed in front of the grandiose Rock of Gibraltar. Beautifully silhouetted against the sky and rising vertically to a height of 1,396 ft (428 m) the Rock was so close to hand, yet out of reach. Owing to a border dispute the road was closed in 1969. Two military units, one British, the other one Spanish, hardly 100 yards apart, each flying its national flag, guarded the barriers. Whilst the British gate was opened every morning, the Spanish gate remained permantently shut. The two flags are just visible in the hazy picture opposite: the Spanish soldier seen leaning on their gate was obviously bored to death, but MMM had only one option: to *turn back*. It was tragic. At the nearby Tarifa MMM was only eight miles from Africa, and at Cap Trafalgar we were 174 years and twelve days too late to hear the roar of guns in the Battle of Trafalgar. MMM completed this grand journey of 3,385 miles (5,416 km) without any difficulties.

MMM IN THE LAND OF WINDMILLS

12 September 1981   Mileage: 127,630

During the second tour of Spain in 1981 MMM went to explore its interior, the region of La Mancha in particular. The flat, fertile and hot area, just south of Madrid, was the domain of the legendary knight, Don Quixote de la Mancha. According to the Spanish novelist Cervantes, it was at Consuegra that Don Quixote spotted his enemies disguised as windmills. There they were, all of the same size and the same shape, equidistantly spaced along the ridge. Ignoring the warnings from his servant Sancho Pancha that these were only windmills, he made a charge at full gallop, his long lance pointing straight at them.

In Persia windmills were known to exist already in the seventh century. The formidable Mongolian conqueror called Gengis Khan — the literal translation being 'Universal Ruler' — took many prisoners of war during his campaigns in Persia. Realising the immense value of windmills as a source of power he ordered all windmillwrights to be sent to China to act as instructors in building windmills for irrigation.

The first windmill in England was built way back in 1187. Many of them were built and remained in use for a long time. They started to fall into decline about a hundred years ago owing to steam power and electricity.

MMM is seen here among the windmills above the village of Campo de Criptana in the La Mancha region. The young man in the bottom picture is the author's right hand, Laurie Green, seen here adding a touch of life to the scene.

84

MMM VISITS THE PROVENCE
25 May 1987   Mileage: 150,675

MMM took part in the fifth European tour organised by the MMOC. To shift 100 Morris Minors and their passengers across the English Channel, send them 650 miles south of Calais, then squeeze them into a camping site without paralysing it, is a major work in the art of co-ordination. In 1987 the MMOC achieved this, and more, because on arrival the British contingent was augmented by Morris Minor brothers and sisters from Denmark, Holland, Norway and Switzerland.

The venue, St Rémy-de-Provence near Avignon, France, was ideal as sunshine, scented air, exquisite food, drink and camaraderie were guaranteed. Following the pattern of previous years only three days out of fourteen had organised events; otherwise it was 'do-as-you-please'. Whether one went to explore Avignon, Marseille, Nîmes or Les Baux, there were dozens of Morris Minors there. Even the French Riviera was within reach. One day, on a trip to see thousands of flamingos in the Rhône estuary, Camargue, MMM came across an ingenious road sign: a giant barrel. There it stood, on a road crossing, advertising the products of the estate of Lausières. Their noble wines were winning gold medals year after year. And, imagine, sixty pence was all they charged for a bottle. The volume of that barrel was such that 12,600 bottles could be filled. Suppose that the barrel was in your cellar and you drank a bottle a day the stock would last 34 years! What Providence has in store for that barrel no one knows but it would not be surprising to see it one day being used as a car garage. Such is Provence!

MMM GOES TO MONTE CARLO

6 June 1987   Mileage: 152,018

I intended to give up motoring early in 1987, the reason being that both of us were a bit old: MMM thirty years and I approaching seventyseven. *But* before parting company with 'my most obedient servant' I felt that a circular tour – London, Monte Carlo, London – would constitute a most appropriate grand finale. To realise this ambition MMM went first for a short holiday with the Club to St Rémy-de-Provence and a week later proceeded alone in stages along the French Riviera towards Monte Carlo.

A glorious blend of sunshine, grand scenery, architectural beauty and culture met MMM already at St Tropez and accompanied it all the way. At Cannes — and later — a balmy breeze, waving palm leaves in MMM's direction, sang softly and incessantly 'Bienvenu, MMM, bienvenu'. This was no figment of imagination. MMM saw it, we heard it and the photograph shows it. At Nice, which is not in vain called 'the Queen of the Riviera', MMM got a highly appreciated present: a regular 1,000-mile service, the clock standing at exactly 152,000.

The territorially small, but in other aspects grand, Principality of Monaco, perched high on the rocks, was entered in triumph. A drive along Monte Carlo's Grand Prix Circuit always makes history for 'man and beast', and so it did in the case of MMM. On the way home, over the French Alps, MMM's performance was perfect, and as I had driven it all the way there and back with the greatest of pleasure and ease, at home a question cropped up: "What to do now? Stop motoring? Dismiss my most obedient servant?"

Dismiss? ... I? ... Never!

A LEGEND IS BORN

No secret forces have to be at work to create a legend. Legends are born, born of casual remarks, conversation and stories based on facts. And this is exactly how the Morris Minor legend has emerged.

In the eyes of many ordinary members of the British population the Morris Minor is regarded as the best British car ever produced. This view has been expressed by thousands of people over and over again. Statements like: "I am sorry I sold mine" … "it never let me down" … "so economical" … "so easy to maintain and repair" … "splendid design" … "excellent workmanship" … "fully British" … "if you wish to sell yours, please, let me know". All of these are the ingredients with which the Morris Minor legend has been construed.

The Morris Minor has never been the 'King of Cars' nor the 'Car of Kings'. It has, however, always been the darling of the British populace, deeply impressed on their minds and firmly imbedded in their hearts. Thousands of lovingly restored Minors confirm this. And MMM's uninterrupted series of thirtythree annual Road Tax Discs is also one of the foundation stones on which part of the Morris Minor legend rests.

MMM FACES UTTER DESOLATION
23 June 1984   Mileage: 138,630

Numerous are the stories about Highlanders abandoning their homes and moving to pastures new. One would think that those days were over. North of Golspie, however, there was a farmhouse with a roofless barn behind it. The house itself appeared to be in reasonable condition, there was even a lamp-post, bulb and all, in front of it, but the tall grass in the drive bore witness that nobody had passed that way for a long, long time. With caution MMM crawled towards the barn, only to find itself face to face with utter desolation. The roof of the barn had caved in, the door was torn off its hinges, and the windowless holes resembled empty eye sockets of some giant blind beast. In the yard decayed farming implements were disintergrating from rust, rot had eaten away half a wheel of a horse cart and high up on the walls were several generations of weeds. On the front door a rusty padlock still guarded the indoor treasures. A peep through the partly-boarded-up window revealed a fully equipped kitchen in disarray, pots, pans and plates on the floor beneath the shelves which had rotted away and broken down. The place had obviously been abandoned. On the kitchen windowsill, however, lay the familiar yellow AA handbook, issue 1963/64. That fact spoke loud enough. It was indeed a quirk of fate that only a few hours previously MMM had visited Dunrobin Castle, the home of one of the richest landowners of his time.

MMM MEETS ITS CREATOR

27 November 1982   Mileage: 132,350

The Morris Minor and Mini were designed by Alexander Issigonis. In recognition of the excellence of his work a knighthood was bestowed upon him in 1969.

In November 1982, MMM was privileged to visit Sir Alec. On our arrival he received us with a friendly expression on his face. This, no doubt, was based on the strong link which existed between him and us: his baby, '79 MMM'. We shook hands cordially. On inspecting MMM he expressed his satisfaction. "Well, well … 25 years old … 132,000 miles … 24 times in Europe … original engine and gearbox … and no trouble! Marvellous! This is how I want it to be." And he gave MMM a pat on the bonnet.

The photographic session was short. Very short. After a couple of shots he ordered: "This is enough". Later, over a glass of sherry, he said that he had stopped granting interviews owing to poor health. So we limited ourselves to answering his questions about trips to Europe, MMOC rallies and links with branches overseas. Before departure he presented MMM with a letter and membership card which he had received from the Norwegian Morris Minor Klubb. That historic visit to Sir Alec is recorded in MMM's logbook in block capitals.

Ten million vehicles were built to the designs of this great man, but small indeed is the number of Morris Minors — and Minis — which received an accolade from Sir Alec for their Twentyfifth Anniversary.

Regretably Sir Alec is with us no longer.

Medl.nr. *A/100*
Navn _*Alec Issigonis*_
Adresse _*England*_
Medlemskontigent
NORDISK MORRIS MINOR KLUBB
Box 37, Hovseter, Oslo 7, Norge
sign...... *Ole Østby* ......

SOME LOG BOOK & DIARY DETAILS

CAR DIARY

LOG BOOK
PART I

Morris Minor 1000
Reg. No 79 MMM

M. Horvat
9 Liston Rd.
LONDON SW4

STARTED JULY 1957

DATE	MILEAGE	
19/7	75	car delivered
"	"	2 gall in tank
21/7	100	2 gall
28/7	200	2 gall
4/8	300	2 gall
16/8	380	engine oil changed 7 pints
18/8	400	4 gall
21/8	550	During the running in period the car did 40 mpg (mostly in town)
22/8	550	2 gall in tank
24/8	600	3 gall (Saffron Walden and Cambridge)

3rd trip abroad: START →
Partner: wife SLAVA; met brother Rudi and Bibjana

TOTAL MILEAGE: 1989 m (3,200 Km)

PETROL CONSUMPTION: 42 gall (192 lit)

average: 47½ mpg (6 lit/100 Km)

1000 m service →

No mechanical trouble

END OF HOLIDAY →

DATE	MILEAGE	1964
28/5	32,000	New water pump £4/4/11
7/6	32,135	4g. Shell Super, Leith Hill
19/6	32,266	4g Esso Extra, tank full
"	32,346	2g Esso Ex, Dover - Ostend
20/6	?	20 l Shell at Koblenz (Germany)
22/6	32,850	25 l EE at ULM, INNSBUCK (Aust) 8 pm
26/6	33,085	20 l BP at Corvara (Italy)
1/7	33,250	20 l at Villach, FAAKER SEA (AUSTRIA)
2/7	33,300	1000 service
3/7	33,430	crossing GROSSGLOCKNER PASS
4/7	33,500	25l at KITZBÜHEL for MUNICH (GERMANY)
4/7	33,750	20 l at KARLSRUHE (GERMANY)
5/7	34,000	17½ l at AACHEN, OSTEND
5/7	34,175	2g EE at Dover
12/7	34,255	5g tank full end of hold.
19/7	34,500	4g Clev. to KERSEY (Suffolk)
26/7	34,700	4g EE BOGNOR REGIS

14 SUNDAY
3rd after Trinity

15 MONDAY

16 TUESDAY *got a new*
☽ First Quarter *passport*
— No 367412

17 WEDNESDAY

18 THURSDAY
Waterloo, 1815

19 FRIDAY *32266 m*
start at 7.20 p.m
good going — in
rain (80 m & Dover) 80

20 SATURDAY *arr. Ostend*
s.r. 3.42, s.s. 8.20 *3:30 a m*
32346 — raining
heavily all the
way / lunch
Cologne — Rest Früh
sleeping
NOTES Aug. Holiday, 7 weeks from June 15
stop at Braubach
arr. Rüdesheim 6 p.m
met Rudi & Bibjan
(306 m) 32652 Drossel

21 SUNDAY *32652 m*
4th after Trinity. Longest Day
Rüdesheim camp
Bad Albach — swimming
resting — visited Nieder-
wald denkmal

22 MONDAY *(32652) left*
camp at 7 a m, to Ulm
non stop — lunch at
Wienerhöften — arr Innsb
at 8p.m. dinner and
concert at Breinö Bell

23 TUESDAY *33,000 left*
Innsbruck at 11 via
Europa brücke — arr
Ortisei 4'30 p.m. car
into garage Seilbahn Sicei
Rifugio Troi' 33070 —

24 WEDNESDAY
S. John Baptist *left Rifugio*
Midsummer Day (Quarter Day) *Troi*
at 7 a m — via Sultner
Schwaige — to Tallinger
in rain — rhododendrons
Rifugio des Alpes Rodella

25 THURSDAY *33070*
○ Full Moon *left Rodella*
9 a.m — via Rifugio Piz
Seteur (closed) — on to
Rifugio Emilio Comici —
lunch — St. Christina by chair
lift Ortisei 33085 — Garden

26 FRIDAY *camp Corvara*
— Passo Campolongo —
photographing flowers
Falzarego — & Nuvolao —
on to Cortina in rain
Camp Rochetta

27 SATURDAY *33120 —*
s.r. 3.45, s.s. 8.21 *left Rochetta*
at 9 a.m. Tre Croci —
walking to Lago Sorapis
and Rifugio Luzzatti
lunch — rain — back to
3 Croci via Misurina
NOTES Aug. Holiday, 6 weeks from June 22
to Rifugio Auronzo
camping at 2.250 m
above sea level (7380 ft
next to Austrians

28 SUNDAY *Walking to*
5th after Trinity *refugio Lavaredo*
on to refugio Locatelli
(Monte Paterno) and
back round Tre Cime

29 MONDAY (33135) *Left*
S. Peter *camp Rifugio Auronzo*
at 7 a.m. descent OK —
Toblach — Innichen. Travel
bridge trouble — Lienz —
Villach — Egg nu Faaker See

30 TUESDAY 33250 *Camp*
and lake very nice. the
morning was cold after
heavy rain at night.
Splendid sunshine.
Window shopping at Villach

1 WEDNESDAY 33270 JULY
Hazy weather — trip
by funicular on to
the Gerlitzen Alm.
Boating on the lake

2 THURSDAY 33290 *took*
☾ Last Quarter *car for service*
bought coffee likör
hat & shoes — lazy
afternoon on the lake
in sun. Evening Tabor

3 FRIDAY 33310 *left*
Faaker See camp at 7.30
via Afritz, Mallstatt,
Heiligenblut, Franz
Josefs Hohe. Grossglockner,
Bruck, Kitzbühel. Walk
on Pasterze" 33492 left

4 SATURDAY 33492 *left*
Schwabische See camp at
9 am via Quinz —
(Hotel Stange) thelstern
München Autobahn
Spanferkel at Hofbrau
House — left München

NOTES Aug. Holiday, 5 weeks from June 29
at 2 p.m. Augsburg
Ulm Stgt (5.30 rain)
Karlsruhe —
Mörfelden, camping

5 SUNDAY 33,829 *Start 8*
6th after Trinity *via Mainz —*
Vis n/c — Bingen —
Koblenz — fine weather.
1/2 chicken lunch near
Remagen. Düren Aachen
Brussels Ostend

6 MONDAY 34173 AT DOVER
then safely and sound
back at home after
midnight — and
back to work in the
finis: 34255 m.

7 TUESDAY

8 WEDNESDAY

9 THURSDAY
● New Moon

10 FRIDAY

11 SATURDAY
s.r. 3.56, s.s. 8.14

NOTES Aug. Holiday, 4 weeks from July 6

HISTORIC HOUSES AND CASTLES
VISITED BY MMM

These are the historic houses and castles which MMM had visited in the course of its life. Their location can best be established by referring to *Historic Houses, Castles and Gardens*. All public libraries have this guidebook in stock. The word 'park' or 'place' as part of a name is used in the sense of 'house'.

Abbotsford

Albury Park

Althorp

Arundel Castle

Audley End

Balmoral

Basildon Park

Bateman's

Beaulieu Abbey

Belvoir Castle

Blair Castle

Blenheim Palace

Blickling Hall

Boughton Monchelsea

Braemar Castle

Breamore

Broadlands

Burghly House

Caernarvon Castle

Compton House

Croft Castle

Castle Howard

Chartwell

Chatsworth House

Chicheley Hall

Chiddingston Castle

Clandon Park

Claydon House

Cliveden House

Cobham Hall

Cuckfield Park

Ditchley Park

Dorney Court

Dunrobin Castle

Dyrham Park

Edinburgh Castle

Eilean Donan Castle

Firle Place

Godinton Park

Goodwood

Ham House

Hardwick Hall

Hatchlands

Hampton Court

Harewood House

Hatfield House

99

continued overleaf

Hever Castle

Highclere Castle

Hughenden Manor

Ickworth

Ightham Mote

Keddleston Hall

Knebworth House

Kingston Lacy House

Knole Castle

Leeds Castle

Leighton Hall

Littlecote

Longleat

Losely Park

Lullingstone Castle

Luton Hoo

Marble Hill House

Mereworth

Osborne House

Osterley Park

Parham Park

Penshurst Place

Petworth House

Pevensey Castle

Preston Manor

Polesden Lacey

Ragley Hall

Rockingham Castle

Rousham Park

Royal Pavillion Brighton

Salisbury Hall

Sandringham House

Sawston Hall

Scone Palace

Sheffield Park

Sherborne Castle

Squerryes Court

Standen

Stonor

Stratfield Saye

Syon House

Traquair House

Uppark

Vyne (The)

Waddesdon Manor

Warwick Castle

Weston Park

Wilton House

Wimpole Hall

Windsor Castle

Woburn Abbey

Wrest Park

West Wycombe Park

MMM'S TWENTYSEVEN EUROPEAN JOURNEYS

A proof of what Morris Minors are capable of enduring.

All journeys started and finished in London.
Codes: A = Austria, B = Belgium, F = France, G = West Germany, H = Holland,
I = Italy, L = Luxemourg, Sp = Spain, Sw = Switzerland.

Date and mileage at start:	ROUTE
1) August 1961 17,100	Dover-Ostend, Cologne (G), Rhine Gorge, Stuttgart, Ulm, Innsbruck (A), Kitzbühel, Grossglockner Pass, Oberammergau (G), Stuttgart, Brussels, Ostend-Dover; 2,170 miles (3,472 km), 51 mpg. Partner (from Stuttgart back to Stuttgart): younger brother Rudi.
2) June 1963 26,350	Dover-Ostend, Stuttgart, Ulm, Neuschwanstein Castle, Innsbruck (A), Brenner Pass (old), Bolzano (I), passes Costalunga, Pordoi, Sella and Falzarego, then Cortina d'Ampezzo, Tre Croci Pass, Rifugio Auronzo, and back via Innsbruck, Oberammergau, Stuttgart, Rhine Gorge, Aachen, Brussels (B), Ostend-Dover; 1,885 miles (3,016 km), 50 mpg. Partner: wife Slava.
3) June 1964 32,266	Dover-Ostend, Rhine Gorge, Ulm, Innsbruck, new Europa Bridge, Brenner Pass, Ponte Gardena (I), Gardena Pass, Corvara, passes Campolongo and Falzarego, Cortina d'Ampezzo, pass Tre Croci, Lake Misurina, Rifugio Auronzo, then back via Lienz (A), Villach, Millstatt Lake, Grossglockner Pass, Kitzbühel, Munich (Autobahn), Ulm, Rhine Gorge, Aachen, Brussels, Ostend-Dover. 1,989 miles (3,200 km) 47½ mpg. Partner: wife Slava.
4) June 1965 39,133	Dover-Calais, Reims, Dôle, Geneva (Sw), United Nations Palace, Lausanne, Martigny, Sierre, Leukerbad, Visp, St Niklaus (Zermatt) and back via Lausanne, Besançon (F), Reims, Laon, Calais-Dover. 1,408 miles (2,252 km) 45 mpg. Partner: wife Slava.
5) March 1966 43,044	Dover-Calais, Amiens, Chantilly, Paris, Boulogne, Cap Griz Nez (starting and/or finishing point for cross-Channel swimmers), Calais-Dover. A full petrol tank plus 20 litres bought in France was enough to get us there and back; 520 miles (832 km) 47 mpg. Partners: wife Slava, daughter Lyerka and Dr Nada Sekolec.

6) End August 1966
45,720

Dover-Calais, Arras, St Dizier, Besançon, Neuchatel (Sw), Bern, Interlaken (camping Manor Farm, excellent), Grindelwald, Lauterbrunnen, back via Bern, Pontarlier (F), Reims, Calais-Dover. 1450 miles (2320 km) 48 mpg. Partners: wife Slava and daughter Lyerka.

7) End April 1967
49,046

Dover-Dunkerque (F), Lille, Charleroi (B), Namur, Luxembourg (L), Worth on Rhine (G), Stuttgart, Wildbad (Black Forest), spa Baden-Baden, Koblenz, Liège (B), Brussels, Ostend-Dover; 1,200 miles (1,920 km) 46 mpg. Partners: wife Slava and daughter Lyerka.

8) September 1967
51,878

Dover-Calais, Reims, Langres, Belfort, Bern (Sw), Interlaken, Grindelwald, Lucerne, Basel, Strasbourg (F), Nancy, Reims, Calais-Dover; 1,637 miles (2,620 km) 48 mpg. Partner: Graham Rendle.

9) June 1968
55,655

Dover-Calais, Cambrai, Sedan, Verdun, Metz, Wörth upon Rhine near Karlsruhe (G), Stuttgart, Basel, Bern, Lucerne (camping Lido splendid), St Gotthard Pass (fog, no views), Stressa on Lago Maggiore (I), back via Domodossola, Simplon Pass (Sw), Brig, Goppenstein-Kandersteg (MMM ferried by train through the tunnel), Bern, Basel, Belfort, Reims, Calais-Dover; 1,685 miles (2,695 km) 47 mpg. Partners: wife Slava and daughter Lyerka.

10) June 1969
61,075

MMM crossing the Channel by air from Lydd to Le Touquet airport (F), Compiègne, Troyes, Langres, Basel, Lucerne, Einsiedeln and back, MMM crossing Lake Lucerne by ferry Gersau-Beckenried, Interlaken, Bern, Basel, Bar-sur-Aube, then MMM flying home from Le Touquet to Lydd; 1,450 miles (2,320 km) 50 mpg. Partners: wife Slava and daughter Lyerka.

11) May 1970
65,850

Dover-Zeebrugge, Brussels, Rhine Gorge, Stuttgart, Munich, Innsbruck, Brenner Pass, Merano (I), St Moritz (Sw), Bernina Pass and back, Julier Pass, Lenzerheide, Chur, Schwyz, Gersau ferry, Interlaken, Wintrösch Alp and back, Reims, Boulogne-Dover; 1,900 miles (3,040 km) 47 mpg. Partner: Sydney Thame.

12) September 1970
68,720

Dover-Boulogne, Amiens, Reims (visit to champagne cellars Pomery and Greno), Tavannes Pass, Biel (S), Interlaken, Grimsel Pass, Martigny, Lausanne, Pontarlier (F), Reims Boulogne-Dover; 1,460 miles (2,335 km) 48 mpg. Partner: Charles Reynolds.

13) September 1971   Dover-Boulogne, Arras, Paris (newly opened Boulevard
    73,625   Peripherique), Geneva, Chamonix (F), Mont Blanc Tunnel,
                     Cervinia and back (I), Great St Bernard Pass (Sw), Martigny,
                     Rhône Valley to Sierre, then high altitude villages Chandolin
                     (6,343 ft/1,934 m), St Luc and Zinal in the beautiful
                     Anniviers Valley; Arolla (6,553 ft/ 1,998 m) in the equally
                     splendid Herens Valley; back to Sion, Furka and Susten
                     Pass, Interlaken, Bern, Pontarlier, Beaune (A6) Paris,
                     Boulogne-Dover. MMM's most arduous journey;
                     1,792 miles (2,867 km) 45 mpg. Partner: Ernest Tavener.

14) June 1972   Dover-Zeebrugge (B), Antwerp, Aachen, Rhine Gorge,
    78,668   Ketsch near Heidelberg, Leonberg near Stuttgart, Brenner
                     Pass, St Magdalena-Glätsch Alp (I), passes Gardena,
                     Campolongo, Falzarego and Mauria to Tolmezzo. Back via
                     Plöcken Pass (A), Lienz, Dobbiaco (I), Brenner Pass,
                     Innsbruck, Telfs, Arlberg Pass, Feldkirch, Principality
                     Liechtenstein, Zürich (Sw), Neuenhof, Waldshut (G), again
                     the source of the Danube at Donaueschingen, Stuttgart and
                     on to Zebrugge. 2,200 miles (3,520 km). 42 mpg (car heavily
                     loaded). Partners: wife Slava, daughter Lyerka and niece
                     Dubravka Vidić.

15) September 1972   Newhaven-Dieppe, Paris, Avalon, Pontarlier, Lausanne,
    81,520   Martigny; then home via Bern, Dôle, Nemours, Paris
                     Dieppe-Newhaven. 1,200 miles (1,920 km). 50 mpg.
                     No partner.

16) September 1973. Newhaven-Dieppe, Paris, Dijon, Lausanne, Martigny,
    86,525   Bagnes Valley and back, Great St Bernard Pass and back,
                     Martigny, Goppenstein-Kandersteg tunnel, Interlaken, Adel-
                     boden and back, Mülenen (Niesenbahn), Bern, Pontarlier,
                     Beaune, Paris, Dieppe-Newhaven. 1,400 miles (2,240 km).
                     48 mpg. No partner.

17) June 1974.   MMM carried a two-seater canoe via Newhaven-Dieppe,
    89,910   Paris (A6), Mâcon, Bourg-en-Bresse to Geneva; MMM
                     visited again the United Nations Palace; during the five-day
                     canoe trip from one end of the Geneva Lake to the other
                     MMM was simply abandoned in a street; MMM collected
                     the canoe from Vevey, then Valorbe, Pontarlier, Beaune,
                     Paris, Dieppe-Newhaven. 1,330 miles (2,130 km). 44 mpg.
                     Partners: Mrs Joy Jones and Anthony.

18) September 1974.
92,117

Newhaven-Dieppe, Paris Beaune, Vevey on Lake Geneva, Rhône Valley to Visp, Saas Fee and back, Grimsel Pass, Interlaken, Lucerne, Waldshut (G), again the source of the Danube at Donaueschingen, Stuttgart, Rhine Gorge, Berleburg near Cologne, Mosel Valley, Luxemborg, Sedan Calais-Dover. 1,872 miles (2,995 km). 45 mpg.
Partner: wife Slava.

19) September 1975.
98,595

MMM took the two-seater canoe again to Lake Geneva, this time for a complete circumnavigation of the lake. Itinerary as in 1974. 1,370 miles (2,200 km). 44 mpg.
Canoeing partner: nephew Hrvoje Horvat from Yugoslavia; otherwise no partner.

20) August 1976.
103,540

Price of petrol 77p per gallon. Newhaven-Dieppe, Lucerne (as in previous years), Neuenhof, Andermatt, Furka Pass, MMM left on the huge car park at Täsch (Zermatt); then home via Lausanne, Paris and Dieppe. 1,482 miles (2,370 km). 48 mpg. This was believed to be MMM's last journey in Europe. No partner.

21) October 1979.
113,360

Newhaven-Dieppe, Chartres (F), Limoges, Carcassonne, Costa Brava (Sp), Benidorm, Granada, Malaga, Torremolinos, Gibraltar, Cadiz, Sevilla, Cordoba, Toledo, Madrid, Burgos, Irun, Biarritz (F), Bordeaux, Chartres, Dieppe-Newhaven. 3,385 miles (5,416 km) in seven weeks. 48 mpg. Partner: Laurie Green.

22) May 1980.
117,800

Dover-Calais, Reims, Gsteig, Vevey, Dijon, Epernay (visited Moët & Chandon's champagne cellars), Reims, Calais-Dover. 1,365 miles (2,185 km). 42 mpg.
Partners: Miss Carol Selby and Laurie Green.

23) September 1980.
120,065

Newhaven-Dieppe, Paris, Gsteig (Sw), Saas Fee, then alone over the Simplon Pass to Stresa, Bologna, Livorno, Rome, and back via Livorno, Genoa, Aosta, Great St Bernard Pass, Bern, Paris, Dieppe-Newhaven. 2,415 miles (3,865 km). 46 mpg, three pints of oil, in four weeks with not a drop of rain. Partner at the beginning of the journey: MMM's strangest passenger, Rovert.

24) September 1981. Newhaven-Dieppe, Le Mans (F), Bordeaux, St Sebastian
    126,300   (Sp), Rioja region, crossed river Ebro (Iber), Logroño,
                         Teruel, Cuenca, La Mancha region, Belmonte, Campo de
                         Criptana, Consuegra, Toledo, Avila, Segovia, Valladolid,
                         Santander, Bilbao, Irun, Biarritz (Fr), Bordeaux, Medoc
                         region, Château Latour, Tours, Chartres, Dieppe-
                         Newhaven. Chasing the winter sun. 3,005 miles (4,808 km)
                         in four weeks. 43 mpg. Partner: Laurie Green.

25) April 1983.   First European tour organised by MMOC. Dover-Calais in
    133,410   the company of 95 Morris Minors; Senlis (F), Fontainbleau,
                         Chablis, Beaune, Château Corton, Clos Vougeot, Château
                         Gevrey-Chambertin, Nuits St George, Troyes, Châlons-sur-
                         Marne, Calais-Dover. The Burgundy region is magnificent.
                         1,125 miles (1,800 km). 49 mpg. With the engine having
                         been rebored not a drop of oil was required.
                         Partner: Laurie Green.

26) May 1986.   Fourth European tour organised by the MMOC. MMM
    145,830   started a week earlier. Dover-Calais, Verdun, Saarbrucken,
                         Zirndorf near Nürnberg, Leonberg near Stuttgart, Karlsruhe,
                         Baden-Baden, Ribeauvillé, Mulhouse and back, Nancy,
                         Calais-Dover. 1,527 miles (2,443 km). 52 mpg.
                         MMM's flattest journey. No partner.

27) May 1987.   Fifth European tour organised by the MMOC. Newhaven-
    150,675   Dieppe, Burgundy region, Beaujolais region, Lyon, Côte du
                         Rhône, St Rémy-de-Provence, Camargue, Avignon, Les
                         Baux, Pont du Gard, Lauzières, Salines de Giraud,
                         St Tropez, Cannes, Nice, Eze, Monte Carlo, Ventimiglia (I),
                         Col de Tende, Colle della Maddalena, Briançon, Col de
                         Lauraret (snowing), Col de la Croix de Fer, Mâcon, Orléans,
                         Versailles, Dieppe. 2,350 miles (3,750 km) in three weeks.
                         50 mpg. Partner: Laurie Green.

THE 1987 TOUR: GRAPH

The graph opposite indicates the altitudes which MMM had to overcome on two of its European tours.

Starting from sea level 'London' in the bottom left-hand corner, moving up to the Bessey Pass, 1,850 ft (565 m), and you have reached the upper slopes of the marvellous vineyards of the Côte d'Or in Burgundy. Coming downwards you land, first, at St Rémy-de-Provence — the venue of MMOC's French tour in 1987 — and just a bit further down you come to the estuary of the river Rhône, called Camargue, which is the marshy home of thousands of flamingos. The climb to Les Baux, a mysterious mediaeval high-cliff village, was steep, but as you see not very high. Now you descend again to the Camargue, this time to see the herds of wild bulls and wild horses. Eze was another charming high-cliff village near the sea, where, before the First World War, a Russian prince had had his castle built. After Eze you are on the French Riviera at Monte Carlo. So far the country was quite hilly, but the entry into Italy via the Tende Pass was very long and steep. And so was the descent into the wine region near Cuneo. Quitting Italy via Maddalena Pass was worse than going over the Tende Pass. The drop into France was pleasant and by the time the Lautaret Pass was reached MMM was in the region of eternal snow and ice of the Savoy Alps. All very beautiful, but hard on MMM. On many an occasion MMM had to run in second gear for half an hour, even longer. After Mâcon the Bessey Pass put us onto the road home. All those climbs amounted to 31,317 ft (9,548 m) which is 2,290 ft more than the height of Mount Everest. To visualise a height of 9,548 metres just imagine ninetynine Big Bens, or sixty Blackpool Towers, or seven Ben Nevises standing on top of each other!

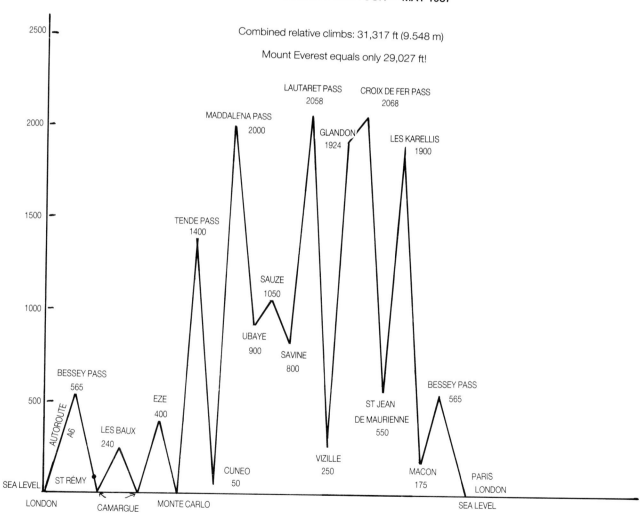

MMM's 27th EUROPEAN TOUR — MAY 1987

Combined relative climbs: 31,317 ft (9.548 m)

Mount Everest equals only 29,027 ft!

MMM's MOST ARDUOUS TOUR: GRAPH

Of all MMM's European journeys its thirteenth, in September 1971, was the most arduous one of all. Due to amazingly fine weather the original modest route was changed beyond recognition and MMM was mercilessly driven on and on, higher and higher. Reading the graph from left to right it becomes clear that the tour started at London, sea level zero. From Paris the autoroute A6 took MMM over the Bessey Pass to the attractive wine-trading town of Beaune, and then on to Geneva. On this stretch it had to cross the chain of the Jura Mountains which separate France from Switzerland. Between the passes of Savine and Givrine there was a deep gap at the market town, Morez.

Everything, so far, was beautiful, but at Chamonix with Mont Blanc within arm's reach, the scenery became truly glorious. As can be seen from the graph the French end of the tunnel is 1,274 metres (4,178 ft) high, and the Italian end even higher (4,526 ft / 1,380 m). At such altitudes the views are always open and grand. To enable us to do a bit of mountaineering in the Matterhorn region MMM had to take us from the town of Aosta to the tourist resort of Breuil (in Italian: Cervinia) and then back again. There we said goodbye to Italy and entered Switzerland via the Great St Bernard Pass. Very hard work it was for MMM, but most rewarding from our point of view. From the Swiss town of Martigny an excursion was made to Chandolin, and later from Sion to Arolla. All this was not a mad rush. There the distances from place to place were not great, but the roads were very steep.

At Sion, after Arolla, the long way home began, first by crossing the Bernese Oberland, then the Jura, to finish with the little hop over the Bessey Pass.

This tour, MMM's most arduous ever, included five mountain ranges: the Jura, the Mont Blanc region, the Matterhorn area, the Bernese Oberland and once more the Jura. This 1,792 miles (2,867 km) long journey involved relative climbs amounting to 13,310 metres (43,670 ft) which is slightly less than the height at which the Concorde cruises. And MMM did it without a single mechanical hitch, just the same as it had done on the previous twelve continental tours.

MMM's MOST ARDUOUS EUROPEAN TOUR (13th) SEPTEMBER 1971
Bernese Alps — partner: Ernest Tavener

Combined relative climbs: 43,670 ft (13,310 m / 8.3 miles)

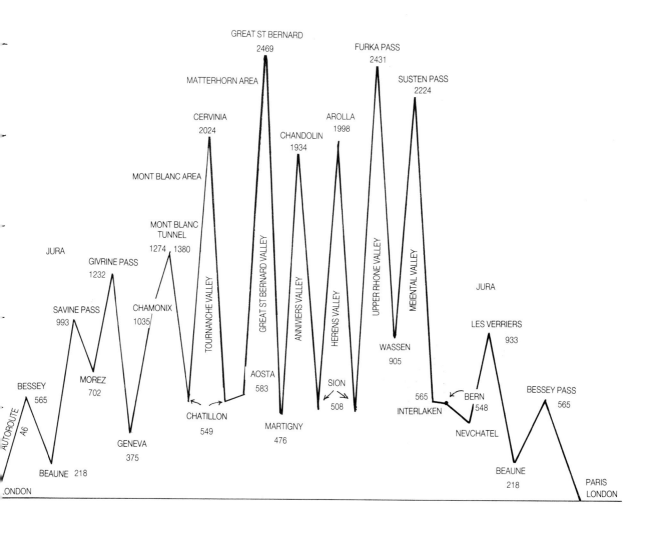

POSTSCRIPT

How long does a car, in fact, last?

The answer can be given either in terms of years, or miles, or by some other method of comparison.

What about MMM?

Seen in the light of some national and world events MMM's life has, so far, covered the terms of office of:

Four Archbishops of Canterbury: G. F. Fisher, A. M. Ramsey, D. F. Coggan and R. A. Runcie, all of them Doctors of Divinity, and all of whom had used as their official transport non other than a Morris Minor, supplied by the Church Commissioners.

Seven Presidents of the USA: Dwight Eisenhower, John F. Kennedy, Lyndon Johnson, Richard Nixon, Gerald Ford, James Carter, Ronald Reagan and the present President, George Bush — none of them interested in Morris Minors.

Seven British Prime Ministers: Harold Macmillan, Sir Alec Douglas-Home, Harold Wilson, Edward Heath, Harold Wilson again, James Callaghan and Margaret Thatcher (a Morris Minor is rumoured to have been Mrs Thatcher's favourite car).

Two wars were fought during MMM's lifetime: a military one, in the Falklands, and a political one in the British coal mines. The former, in 1982, broke out when MMM's mileage stood at 129,800 and ended with 130,300 miles on the clock. Thus, from MMM's point of view, that war lasted only 500 miles, and indeed it was short. The enmities ceased after two-and-a-half months. The story of the latter, however, was different. It broke out with 137,300 miles on the clock and ended with 141,400. So according to MMM, the Miners' Strike lasted 4,100 miles and that was indeed a lengthy affair — from March 1984 to March 1985.

Famous people who departed this world during MMM's lifetime are too many to quote. But three names stand out: on the national scene that of Sir Winston Churchill (died January 1965) and on the Morris Minor horizon those of William Richard Morris, later Lord Nuffield (died 1963) and Sir Alec Issigonis (died 1988).

In the world of industry and commerce the changes were many. I would quote only two cases: the Morris Car factory at Cowley near Oxford exists no longer. Now it is the Rover Group. And the once famous London Distributors of Morris Cars, Stewart & Arden, do not exist now, either.

110

Of the many who, like MMM, are still going strong I again wish to mention only two instances: H. M. The Queen. At the time when MMM had left the factory assembly lines the Queen had been five years on the Throne. Now it is the thirtyeighth year of her reign. May she live long. The other instance is Agatha Christie's theatre thriller *The Mousetrap* which is also in its thirty-eighth year — a world record.

When production ceased and the spare parts situation became precarious, Morris Minors showed signs of becoming an endangered species. However, the Morris Minor Centre at Bath under the guiding light of Charles Ware succeeded in breathing life into that sector. Now even a Morris Minor Series Three is planned. In addition to this, a number of specialist firms came into existence.

Thus there is every hope that Morris Minors will last into the Third Millenium. They well deserve this because it was they who made the image of the British Car Industry shine a good deal more brightly. And I sincerely hope that MMM, irrespective of the owner in whose hands it is going to be, will also be among them.

MORRIS MINOR BIBLIOGRAPHY

Title	Author	Publisher	Category
Autocar (Reprinted Articles)		Temple Press	Technical
Morris Minor 1948-1970 (Reprinted Articles)		Brookland Books	Technical
Marina to Minor (2nd edition)	Burton, Owen	Owen Burton	Technical
The Morris Motor Car	Edwards, Harry	Moorland Publishing	Technical
Morris Minor 1000 Owners Handbook		Haynes Publishing Group	Technical
Morris Minor 1000 Owners Workshop Manual		Haynes Publishing Group	Technical
Super Profile Series (1) *Series MM Morris Minor*	Newell, Ray	Haynes/Foulis	Technical
(2) *Morris Minor and 1000*	Newell, Ray	Haynes/Foulis	Technical
Guide to Purchase and D.I.Y. Restoration of Morris Minors	Porter, Lindsay	Haynes/Foulis	Technical
The Cars of BMC	Robson, Graham	Motor Racing Publications	Historic/Technical
The World's Supreme Small Car (3rd edition)	Skilleter, Paul	Osprey	Historic/Technical
The Durable Car Ownership	Ware, Charles	Morris Minor Centre, Bath	Technical
The Himalayan Minor	Young, Phillip	Speedwell Books	Racing/Rally

---

Minor Matters bi-monthly magazine, published by the Morris Minor Owners Club   Mostly technical

---

Morris Minor Owners Club officials:
Chairman: JOHN FRYE, 'Newholme', The Street, Brampton, nr Buxton, Norfolk NR10 5AA
Secretary: RAY NEWELL, 84 High Street, Loscoe, Derbyshire DE7 7LF
Secretary (membership): Mrs JANE WHITE, 127-129 Green Lane, Derby DE1 1RZ

(When writing to MMOC a S.A.E. is essential).